WHAT EVE
TO RATSY PATSY?

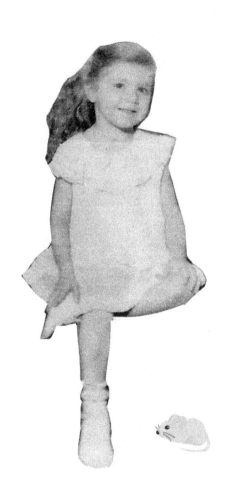

By Patricia Thomas

(me @ 3 yrs old)

WHAT EVER HAPPENED TO RATSY PATSY?

Patricia Thomas

CONTENTS

INTRODUCTION

You are probably wondering about the title, "What Ever Happened to Ratsy Patsy?" It's a name given to me by one of the very young boys who lived in our neighborhood in Detroit during the early 40's. Every time I went to their house to call for my girlfriend to come out and play, her little brother who was about 5 would answer the door and say "well if it isn't Ratsy Patsy". His Father plays a part in one of the stories I will be relating to you in a chapter in this book.

Now that we have that explanation, I just want you to know the real purpose of this book is to give honor and glory to God the Father, God the Son, and God the Holy Spirit. If it were not for the intervention of God in my life, I wouldn't be here writing this book -so thank you God for all You have done for me and my family our whole lives.

I can't tell you the number of times God has helped me. If I'm undecided about something, I ask for His help again and sure enough, He's there for me. In previous years, I would never have even thought about that type of thing, but as I get older (and more forgetful – don't tell anyone I said that), I need His help on a daily basis. I'm pleased to tell you that He gives it to me. Sometimes not the way I expect and not necessarily when I expect it, but always when I really need it, He's there. You might want to try having conversations with God, you might be surprised how He can help you.

Additionally, I want to explain that all events presented in this book actually took place. I did not embellish, exaggerate or improvise any of it. All events are related as best as I can remember. They are not necessarily in the context of chapters, some stories are only one page long, but no less important than those that are 2 or more pages. They are etched in my memory, and when I reread what I have written, I am in awe of the power of Almighty God and the love and care He has for me and my family. Thank you so much Lord!

Now turn the page and let's get on with this book.

ACKNOWLEDGMENTS

There are 4 people to whom I am most grateful and would like to acknowledge that at this time.

1. My Mom was something else. During WW II when my sister and I were growing up, she worked in an airplane factory as a rivet inspector. Even through she worked every day, she still took care of us and our needs. She took us to Church every Sunday ever since I can remember. People always ask me when I was converted to Christianity. I can never answer that question satisfactorily as I've always gone to Church, and always believed in God. I started going to Parochial school in the 6th grade. Prior to that time I attended public school. Public school was a lot different then. Our teachers forever quoted the Golden Rule to us. That wouldn't happen in today's public school. I'm sure my

Mom had to sacrifice in order to pay for the private schools. As my sister also attended Parochial high school at the same time, things could not have been financially that easy for her but we never heard her complain. She wasn't a complainer, she was a doer. If something needed to be done, you could always count on her. We always celebrated the religious holidays and attended Church each Sunday. My Mom was a great example of a person with tenacity. She stuck with things through thick and thin, and even though she's in Heaven, I still admire the way she raised my sister and myself. When my sister was a teenager and I was pre-teen, she remarried and went on to have another family. They were brought up with the same values and self-sacrificing attributes. We always thought of ourselves as sisters, and that's what we were and are to this day. I never heard my Mom swear or speak ill of other people. Believe me, that's not that easy to do. She was not the type of person to gossip about anyone else. She never articulated her feelings about this type of thing, she just lived it. Thank you Lord for such a Great Mom in fact, I and my sisters thank you Lord for a Great Mom!

2. I had been working for an Architect in Newport Beach for almost 8 years. For reasons of his own, he decided to cut

back on personnel and hours. As I was the secretary of the office and handled all the paperwork, my job was not in jeopardy but my hours were cut to 4 hours a day. Unfortunately, I could not afford that to happen. I did something I have never done before - when one of my boss's friends called I asked him if he knew of someone looking for a secretary. To my amazement he said he did, and that was how I came to the office where I am still employed after 23 years. The best part of the office was an Architect named Steve. He was a great Christian and he and I started many conversations regarding that subject. Fortunately for me, he had been brought up in a faith that allowed the reading of the Bible, etc. My Church did not allow the reading of the Bible at all, we didn't even have one in our home when I was growing up. I had no idea there were 66 books in the Bible. I thought there was only Matthew, Mark, Luke and John as most sermons were referenced as being from those Disciples. I had never heard of the Book of Revelation, the Rapture, the Tribulation or the Millennium. Steve told me all sorts of things, and I was overjoyed to learn all of this information. He was very active in his Church and I applauded him for that. Whatever I did not understand, he patiently explained it to me and prayed for me more than once. I started to think about all these things, and decided I needed to become what I hoped would be a better and more knowledgeable Christian. Thank you Lord for Steve.

3. The third person is a lady whose name is Joy, and the name suits her perfectly. I met Joy when I became the responsible party for my Aunt who was 90 at that time. My Aunt lived in Las Vegas (she passed away at 99) and my husband, Larry and I went there as often as we could to handle affairs that could not be resolved from here in California. Joy was in a group from her Church who visited the elderly and helped with their problems, such as doctor visits, etc. My Aunt had fallen while walking (she was 90 and walked 2 miles a day) and was taken to a hospital. She had no I.D. on her and was admitted as Jane Doe. One of her neighbors missed her and called the Police. They came out to her mobile home and discovered she wasn't there. They started contacting hospitals in the area and found an elderly lady had been admitted that morning. Her neighbor went to the hospital and identified her. We were notified and went to pick her up when she was released from the hospital almost a week later. That's when we all met Joy. She has been a true angel of mercy for my Aunt. When Joy remarried she chose a man with her same generous, caring qualities. What a pair they make. They are

such good Christians, so helpful and giving of their time and energy. God truly must have a special place in Heaven for them. I'm very thankful to have she and Abe as friends. Thank you Lord for Abe and Joy.

4. The fourth person for whom I am thankful on a daily basis is Dr. David Jeremiah who is on the radio and TV. He makes the Bible come alive. He's so informative, explains things in a manner that's so easy to understand. I get his books and Study Guides and read something out of one of them each night. I tape his Sunday services so I can watch them again and again. He has a way of relaying information to which you can relate. It's not really preaching, to me it's informing me of things in the Bible that may not always be as clear and understandable as I would like. I order special programs and send them to Joy and Abe as they have Bible studies in their Church for Seniors and young people. Feedback from her has been that the attendees just love the videos, and some people have even accepted Christ as their Savior. What a blessing! He has a website: David Jeremiah. org. Thank you Lord for Dr. David Jeremiah! We are all so blessed by this Pastor.

IN THE BEGINNING

The beginning is always a good place to start so let's do that. In March of 1936 there was a flood in Edwardsville, Pennsylvania as was the usual pattern during the latter part of the Winter, early Spring. On March 17th, my Mom knew I would be arriving very soon, but she couldn't get down into town to the hospital because of the flood. Fortunately, the doctor lived further up the hill and so he walked down to our house and delivered a baby girl, me. Being St. Patrick's day, I'm sure you can guess that's why my name is Patricia.

My Father was a coal miner in one of the mines in that town. I'm not sure how well he enjoyed being a miner, but a cave-in soon encouraged him to change his occupation. Consequently, we moved to Detroit when I was six months old. At first we lived with my aunt, but moved into our own home when I was three. It was a very nice neighborhood, but as my Father was very anti-social it soon became apparent that we were not well-liked as a family. Children especially seem to be able to sense these things as some of the neighbors made that very apparent to me in several ways. My Mother, however, was a good Christian and never spoke ill of my Father nor any neighbor. My sister and I were taken to Church and attended parochial school. I can't remember when I didn't believe in God. I know many people have "conversion stories" but I don't. I remember attending Church on Sundays and worshipping the Lord.

Now that you have a rudimentary background view of my very early childhood, let's move on to a few years later.

TONSILS, NOW YOU HAVE THEM, NOW YOU DON'T

In the early 40's taking out children's tonsils was considered a necessity. So when I was six years old it was decided that my tonsils would be removed. My Aunt and I went to the hospital together and had our surgery on the same day. My Aunt went home the next day but I wasn't able to because my throat wouldn't stop bleeding. Finally, I went back into the operating room and they did something to stop the bleeding. By this time I evidently lost quite a bit of blood. I remember my Mom had to put a kitchen towel under my arms, and help me walk from room to room when I got home from the hospital. I had lost so much blood you could see through the tips of my fingers. I don't remember this but my Mom told me about it years later. Up to this point it pretty much sounds like any other tonsillectomy experience, except for the results of that surgery years later.

When Larry and I had been married a number of years we decided to celebrate one of our anniversaries by going to Hawaii. We decided on a tour of 4 islands. The big day arrived and we departed for sunny Hawaii. I hadn't flown very much at this point, and I was so excited to be flying to Hawaii I could hardly sleep the night before we departed. Our first stop was Maui where we spent 2 days, our next stop was the big island of Hawaii where we spent 2 days. By the time we were on our way to our 3rd stop I had pretty much lost my equilibrium. Larry had to help me up and take me from place to place to sightsee. I was really miserable. When we got home I needed help to get up and down or walk somewhere in the house. The first day Larry went back to work but I was not able to go back to work. Unfortunately, during the day I needed to get up. When Larry got home from work he found me lying on the bathroom floor as I was not able to stand up. We decided it was time to go see our family physician who examined my throat. He asked me to tilt my head back as far as I could on the examining table. He suggested I see an ENT (ear, nose and throat specialist) who decided I needed a Menier's Test. The test revealed that

I had a nonfunctioning Eustacian tube on my right side. It was determined that when I had my tonsils removed, the doctor cut too close on the right side of my throat and almost cut my jugular vein. When the wound healed it pulled the Eustacian tube which twisted and became non-functioning. The ENT doctor told me that ordinarily I would be dizzy as though I had 3 drinks, however, since it happened when I was six years old, my body adjusted to the situation and I was not aware of being dizzy. I do know that it is very difficult for me to fly, move my head quickly from side to side, or a number of other things that would ordinarily make your head spin. Through new type of testing I have just learned that I have Benign Paroxysmal Positional Vertigo, or BPPV. As I get older I find that I'm more aware of being dizzy than I did as a youngster and young adult. Fortunately, in the last number of years doctors have decided the body needs its tonsils, and so they aren't routinely removed as they once were. Thank goodness.

Several years ago my ENT doctor advised me to have tubes surgically inserted in my ears to help with the dizziness and have more equalization of pressure in my head. So we proceeded to do just that. I had 5 sets put in at different times. I could always tell when one or both fell out of my eardrums as I immediately became very dizzy. One time I evidently got some water behind the tube which caused an infection. I had to go to the hospital where my doctor removed the tube, suctioned out the infection, and proceeded to insert a new tube. When I woke up in the recovery room I immediately put my hand to my right ear as it hurt. The nurse in the recovery room noticed my action and came over to me and asked if I was having pain in that ear. I replied I was, and she proceeded to go get me a shot which she said would help alleviate the pain. I was too groggy to ask her what she was going to give me, and rolled over on my side as instructed so she could give me the shot. Within a few seconds I began to have trouble breathing, my throat was beginning to close, and my chest felt as through it was on fire. The nurse came right over to me when she saw my discomfort. She looked at my chart which was at the foot of the gurney, and said, "Oh no, you're allergic to codeine and I gave you a codeine shot". She ran very quickly to get a doctor who came back with a syringe and gave me another shot to counteract the codeine shot. Within a few minutes I began to feel better, but I thought it best to ask what you are receiving as medication no matter where you are. It could be very dangerous other-wise. All of this just because of a tonsillectomy. Thank you

Lord for your watchful eye when the doctor almost cut my jugular vein. You certainly stopped the procedure before it was too late. Thank you again.

YOU WANT HOT WATER, YOU GOT IT

As I previously explained, my parents bought a new house in a very nice neighborhood in Detroit when I was three. Although it was a new house, it was equipped with what was currently available on the market at the time, I'm referring to the water heater. The water heater was in the basement and you had to open up the cylinder-type door, turn on the gas valve, and light it yourself. The big problem with that was you had to remember to turn it off when the water was hot. My Mom had a penchant for turning it on but forgetting to turn it off. Since my Mom worked, my sister and I were latchkey kids. I was approximately 7 or 8 years old and my sister was 7 years older than I. She usually only came home from school around dinner time, consequently I was the first one home. On several occasions I would open

8

the front door only to hear very strange sounds coming from the basement. The first time it happened I opened the basement door and went downstairs only to be met with steam pouring out of pipes, and the pipes themselves sounding as if they would explode. Scared me silly. I ran up the stairs and out the front door as I thought the house was going to explode. I sat on the step outside and was crying as I didn't know what to do. Here is the part where Mr. Fischer, our neighbor whose son called me Ratsy Patsy, comes in. Mr. Fischer came walking down the street toward our house and stopped and asked me why I was crying. I told him and he ran inside (I assume to turn off the gas valve), and opened up all the faucets inside and outside the house. When all the hot water was dispensed, he shut everything off, told me all would be o.k., and went back home. This happened several times, and I now firmly believe that God would send Mr. Fischer on a "walk" which would take him by our house just at the right time. Now you have to understand why I say this, Mr. Fischer was not in the habit of taking walks. He only seemed to take a walk when I needed help.

One time I was sitting on the step crying (this was before Mr. Fischer came walking by) and my Aunt drove up in the driveway. I saw my Mom in the car so I started running toward the passenger door and my Aunt yelled out, "you're not coming with us". I tried explaining about the water heater but she wouldn't listen, and just backed up and out of the driveway. I went back to the step and started crying again, and God sent Mr. Fischer on a "walk" again. Once more he went down the basement to shut off the gas valve and drain all the hot water. Thank you Lord for Mr. Fischer! As a finish to that story, my Aunt and Mom eventually did come back from shopping, and I explained to her why I was running toward the car. She felt just terrible and hugged me and said she was sorry. Yes, eventually my Mom remembered to turn off the gas. But it sure was great when one of those new fangled automatic hot water heaters was installed. Ahhhhhh, isn't progress great! Oh, and thank you Lord for sending Mr. Fischer to help me out again. But I sure was glad about the new automatic water heater!

MURDER ON HIS MIND

Possibly one of the most frightening things to happen to me was at age 8 (this was in the middle 40's). My Mom was very ill with what we would now call the flu but at that time it was called "the Grip". When I came home from school and was playing outside with one of my friends, I noticed a man following us up and down the sidewalk. My friend was riding her tricycle and I was walking beside her. When we finally stopped in front of my friend's house, he also stopped. I looked up at him and saw such evil in his eyes it frightened me. I encouraged my friend to continue riding her bike down to my house. He didn't follow. That night, after it was dark, my aunt came over to see if she could help my Mom. At this time, my Father worked nights and was not at home. About an hour after coming into the house from playing outside, my aunt told me to go to the drugstore and get my Mom a glass straw as she couldn't even sit up to drink any liquids. No, straws were not sold in the stores as they are today. My first reaction was to say that I didn't want to go to the store as it was already dark outside. She became very agitated with me and insisted that I go. She put the money in my pocket and showed me the door. I slowly opened the screen door and looked up and down the street. I knew that man was somewhere out there waiting for me. I cautiously stepped out onto the porch and walked down the 2 steps to the sidewalk. We lived in the middle of a long block with a streetlight in the front of our house by the curb. I started to walk in the direction of the store. When I had gone about 3 houses down from ours, I saw him standing on the corner under the streetlight at the intersection. I didn't know what to do. I couldn't go back home and tell my aunt about him, I knew her well enough to know that she would say I was making the whole thing up just so I wouldn't have to go to the store. I swallowed nervously and continued walking toward that corner with my heart pounding. When he saw me coming down the street he quit leaning against the streetlight, straightened up, and watched me as I walked toward him. I was so scared I didn't know what to do. I knew if I walked past him he would grab me and that would be the end. I don't know how this plan developed in my mind (except for God). I decided, when I got to the corner, I would cross diagonally to the other side of the street. He was waiting on my side of the street where I should have crossed to get by him. When I got to the corner, I suddenly ran diagonally across the street, and he started to move quickly to where I was running. I ran as fast as I could, and he soon quit coming as he knew I had to return home from wherever I was going.

I arrived at the drugstore, purchased the glass straw, and headed out the door of the store. I slowly started walking back the same way I had come trying to think what I should do. I reasoned out that if I went home down the alley it would be very dark and I was almost as afraid of the dark alley as I was of him. Also, he would see me going that way and follow me down the alley. I then thought of returning by the next street but I knew he would cut me off before I could get to my home, and so that idea was quickly discarded. I took a deep breath and continued walking back the same way I had come. I did, however, cross to the other side of the street when I left the drugstore, not the side where he stood waiting for me. As I walked around the curve there he was under the streetlight, waiting for me. The only thing I could think of to do was to cross diagonally as I had done before. So that's what I started to do, however, this time he started to cross to the side where I was. I stopped and that must have caught him off guard for a moment. As he stopped to wonder what I was going to do, I started running diagonally as I had done before. When I reached the other side I ran as fast as my legs would go. Something in my head said, don't look down and don't look back as you will trip and fall. So I did just that, I just keep on running as fast as I could. I did have to travel halfway down this long block, but there was nothing else for me to do but that. I could hear him running behind me as his feet slapped down hard on the pavement. It sounded as though he was very close, but I remembered what I now believe to be God's words not to look down or look back. I reached my house and cut across the lawn and up the steps and opened the screen door. In those days people didn't lock their doors until bedtime, so that was very fortunate for me. As I opened the screen door and turned the knob of the front door he caught up with me, and grabbed the back of my blouse. I wiggled as hard as I could and he lost his grip, I opened the door and went inside. I handed the straw to my aunt and went into my bedroom, sat on the bed and shook for about a half hour. No, I did not tell anyone what had just happened, as I previously said, in those days children were not very often believed. Knowing my aunt, I knew she would say it was just because I didn't want to go in the first place. To my recollection, I didn't tell anyone of this incident until I was in my late 30's. However, I do believe in my heart that if it wasn't for God giving me directions, advice, and the strength to run as fast as I did, I wouldn't be here today. I knew that man had something in mind for me, and it was not good. I was approximately 8, maybe 9 when that incident occurred, and he continued to peek in our windows until we finally moved to another home when I was 15 years old. The reason he could peek into our house, whether it was the bedroom, living room windows or kitchen windows is because my Mom always kept the drapes and blinds open. She knew nothing of the incident and obviously had no reason to close the windows, drapes and blinds. Also, we didn't have air conditioning or fans at that time, and Detroit can be very hot and humid both day and night in the Summer. Our bedroom window was left open all night long as had been the practice for years. My older sister and I shared a bedroom in which there was a double bed. The bed was pushed up in the corner of the room right under the window. Being the younger sister, I was given the order to sleep next to the window. The window was left open, and the shades were not drawn because of the heat and humidity. I often wonder if that man peeked into our window during the night while we slept. My sister was an extremely sound sleeper, and my Mom always kidded her about being so difficult to wake up. It gives me the chills to realize that all he had to do was take the screen off and drag me out the window. I don't think anyone would have heard him. But I do know I can thank God that never happened. I can honestly tell you that I do not go out by myself at night, ever. I also close all blinds and drapes as soon as it starts to get dark. All windows & doors are closed and locked each night be it Summer or Winter here in California. We do have ceiling fans in each room and air conditioning should that be necessary. This probably sounds like I'm paranoid, but I will remember that man until my dying day, and what would have happened to me had he caught me and been able to get me away from my house.

I was thinking about this situation as I was writing it and a thought came into my mind. If that man had crossed the street to the other corner on the same side of the street before I returned from the store, he would have caught me as I tried to diagonally cross to that corner. I had no choice as our house was on that side of the street. Isn't that an interesting thought?

Thank you Lord for the strength to have escaped him and his intentions. I pray he never hurt some other child or adult.

ROLLER SKATES AND ROLLER COASTER

My friends and I loved to roller skate at the roller skating rink. We all were either preteen or in our very early teens. The rink was located some miles from our home so we would take the bus to go skating. One particular Saturday, most of my friends didn't go except for Madlyn and myself. My Mom very specifically told me not to go on any rides as I left the house. She said that because the roller rink was located inside an amusement park. That Saturday, Madlyn and I finished our skating and as we left the rink she said, "Why don't we ride the roller coaster". I hesitated but then agreed to do that. I hadn't ever been on a roller coaster for to tell you the truth it scared me. We went to that section of the park and waited for the ride to begin. We didn't sit in the very front car but chose to sit in one of the middle cars.

During this period of time there were no "seat belts" so to speak, but just a grab bar that ran across the back of the seat in front of you. We both hung onto the bar as the coaster very slowly climbed up that first big hill. As it reached the top and started down, the momentum caused my glasses to fall off as I put my head in a downward position. I let go of the bar to catch them. Since we were heading downward at quite a speed, that particular angle threw me forward and that forced me to stand up. As I stood up, the upper half of my body was pitched forward into the car in front of us. My legs were up on the back of the seat and my hands were gripping the seat of the car in front of ours. My friend thought I was going to fall out, so she stood up and grabbed my ankles and held on for dear life. We stayed in those positions the entire ride, up and down hills, around curves and so on. Finally the ride came to an end and the car stopped at the station. The gentleman taking the tickets came running over to us and started screaming what idiots we were, and he couldn't understand how we didn't fall to the ground. We were both shaken and decided it was not a good idea to tell any family member about what we had done. In retrospect however, to this day I remember my Mom telling me not to go on any rides, she had never said that to me before. But I thank

God for keeping two errant youngsters in those cars, and not falling to the ground where I'm sure we both would have been badly injured or killed. Our Guardian Angels worked overtime that day.

OH MY ACHING HEAD!

One Christmas Eve in 1951 my sister, I, and my brother-in-law arrived back at our house after attending Midnight Mass. My brother-in-law Bill was in the Army and home on leave. As we walked in the door, we saw two young men in uniform sitting on the sofa with my Mom and Dad. It seems that the brothers, Larry and Gordon, had grown up knowing my brother-in-law and all were home on leave at the same time. (This occurred during the Korean War). Larry found out where Bill and my sister were staying and decided to visit on Christmas Eve. Larry and I became good friends and exchanged letters while he was in New York or out on patrol. Larry was in the Coast Guard when I met him, I was 15 and very impressionable. He remained in the service until he was discharged due to a terrible accident 2+ years later. He was stationed on Staten Island, New York, but spent much of his time on a ship which was out of port for 2-3 months at a time. One week near the end of his enlistment, he decided to drive his brother's motorcycle home for the weekend to visit me. First he had to hitch hike to Massachusetts to get the bike. His brother was in the Coast Guard as well, but was on a ship that was out to sea in the North Atlantic. He said the bike didn't run very well on the trip back and he decided he must repair the wiring problem before he could make the trip to Michigan on the bike. He was allowed to park the bike at a Chief Petty Officer's house on the island and worked on it there. Shortly before he was to leave, he thought he would check it out to make sure it was in shape for the trip. It was almost dark when he finally finished checking and fixing and thought he would take the bike out for a test run. When returning to the Chief's house, he had to travel uphill on which was a sign warning: No Parking – Blind Curve Ahead. He noticed the limbs of a Weeping Willow tree hanging about eye level over his lane at the curve. He was driving approximately 10 miles an hour. Unfortunately, a black car was illegally parked just beyond the hanging limbs of the tree. As Larry could not see the car because of the darkness and the limbs, he hit the back of the car, flew over it and hit the pavement with his head and shoulder. Unfortunately, no one wore helmets in those days and Larry didn't have one on either. Fortunately for him a police officer was following a way behind him as the officer was going home for the day. When the officer saw Larry hit the car and fly over it he sped up, and had already called for an ambulance by the time he got to where Larry was lying on the pavement. The ambulance soon arrived and they put him on a stretcher in the back. They had checked all his vital signs and determined that he was deceased. One of the paramedics sat in back with the body as they were on their way to the morgue. Suddenly he saw the sheet flutter, and yelled for the driver to get to the nearest hospital as "this guy is still alive". Once they found out he was a serviceman he was transported to the Maritime Hospital on Staten Island. I knew none of this as there was no reason for the hospital to call me, but they did call his Mother. They told her he had been unconscious for 4 days and they really did not know if he would ever wake up. She called me and asked if I wanted to go with her to New York and see him. My older sister offered to drive us there, it was a nail biting trip. We finally arrived and went directly to the hospital. To everyone's amazement, Larry had just woke up after 4 days of being unconscious, the hospital staff were very pleased, and so were we. We had really expected to be saying goodbye instead of hello to him. Later we found out he had a broken neck in addition to having cracked his skull in 4 places, had a concussion, broke his nose and his collarbone, as well as other cuts and bruises. When we brought him home weeks later he seemed o.k. Years later he said he couldn't even remember anything for about 4-5 days after he emerged from the coma. 50 years later when Larry had a mini-stroke he had an MRI of his skull. The doctor found that the area of his brain where he had hit the pavement (the area over his left eye) was receded and completely dead. I asked the doctor about that area of the brain and he told us that was the memory area. In retrospect, I do remember after the accident Larry couldn't remember some things about himself. The doctor said the body is great as his memory rerouted itself somewhere else in his brain.

Obviously Larry was not meant to die in that accident, the Lord had other plans for him as we got married a few years later, and went on to have a lovely family. We now have been married for 55 years. Thank you again Lord for sparing his life.

Larry has had the Lord watching over him for years, even before he realized that. One such incident happened when he was 7 years old. He and his family lived in a one story house in St. Clair Shores, Michigan. Larry and his older brother, Phil, shared a bedroom with two twin beds. Each bed had a brass headboard. One night Larry was sleeping but his brother was awake and reading. There was a thunderstorm brewing outside, and lightning evidently struck the house. A lightning bolt bounced off of the brass headboard of Larry's bed which elevated him several feet in the air and rotated his body in a circle. As he rotated in the air, the blanket wrapped completely around his body. When Phil ran over to check him to see if he was injured, Larry told him to "go away, I'm sleeping". No ill effects from the lightning – amazing!

Several weeks earlier, Larry and his brother, Phil were walking down the country road on the way to the store. They were walking against traffic as they had been taught to do when there are no sidewalks. Larry was the one closest to the road with Phil on the other side of him. A car hit Larry and both he and Phil were elevated several feet off of the ground. Phil had been holding onto Larry's hand as he was the "younger" brother, and it was dark already. The man who hit Larry was inebriated but he did stop and pick up Larry and Phil. As Larry was unconscious, he put him in the trunk of the car and was driving to the doctor's. The trip was interrupted by a police car that stopped the driver. The officer took Larry out of the trunk and transported he and Phil to the doctor's office. The accident occurred on Easter Eve, and Larry proudly said when he woke up the next day, he had the largest Easter basket. Don't know if you can call that compensation or not – depends on your point of view and your age. At 7, I guess Larry thought that was great! Evidently no ill effects from that accident either – amazing!

When Larry was 15 he and his brothers were seated in the back of a stake truck on their way to being driven to the movies. Larry was sitting next to the back of the truck. He fell asleep and fell out of the truck when it hit a bump. How that went unobserved, I don't know. When the vehicle arrived at the movies is when they missed him. Everyone climbed back into the truck, retraced their steps (so to speak) on the same route as taken when going to the movies. They found him lying at the entrance to a closed market where he had crawled after hitting the road. He had 3 broken front teeth as he had hit his face on the gravel road when he fell out of the truck. Fortunately, he hadn't broken any bones, only front teeth. Larry's Guardian Angel must have worked overtime while he was growing up.

In later years when we moved to California, Larry worked for refrigeration/Air Conditioning contractors. One day he was in a restaurant working on the refrigerator. He was working with the condensing unit which had the protective cover removed from an electrical control. He put both his arms around the unit trying to move it forward and came in contact with the hidden control wiring. He got an electrical shock of about 480 volts which left deep burns on the inside of his right arm. The left arm was grasping the grounded frame, and he was held there by the electrical current. He pushed to break free from the unit with his feet. When he finished the job and went out front, the Manager of the restaurant asked him if he had hurt himself. Larry asked why, and was told by the Manager that he and the patrons heard a very loud scream from the kitchen area. Everyone in the restaurant wondered what had happened. Larry explained in less technical terms what had happened. Everyone was happy he was o.k. It's most fortunate he didn't die from getting electrocuted. Larry's Guardian Angel was working overtime again.

When Larry was 46 or 47 he went to work for one of the large cities here in Southern California. He worked in the HVAC Department. One day he was supervising two men on the removal of a piece of duct work for system improvements. They were near the top of a free standing 16' ladder trying to pull apart duct work. The duct work didn't budge, so Larry climbed the ladder, and assuming there was a hang-up in the duct work he gave it a good pull. It immediately came loose and he slammed his left elbow backwards into a metal beam. Within several hours his upper arm and elbow began to swell. The City sent him to the hospital to check on the injury. They drained the fluid buildup out of his elbow and thought it would be just fine. Unfortunately, every time they drained it, the swelling would return and they would send him back to the doctor. After four attempts to correct the swelling, the surgeon informed him they would have to remove the bursa in his elbow. The bursa is like a cushion in the elbow area, and it must have been injured more than they thought as it just kept filling with fluid. Surgery was scheduled and performed. When Larry woke up from the surgery his arm was in a cast-like bandage which he was to leave on until the next doctor's appointment. When they removed the bandage they discovered he had a staphylococcus infection in that elbow resulting from the surgery. They put him on antibiotics but it didn't seem to help, and he also had Whirlpool treatments. The staph infection just kept getting worse. He had several more surgeries because the infection had progressed to Osteomyelitis. I understood that meant the staph infection just kept eating away at the bone in his elbow. We were even afraid they might have to amputate his arm above his elbow to keep the staph from spreading any more than it had. An infectious disease specialist was called in, and he decided Larry should be in the hospital in isolation until some improvement was evident. I went to see him everyday and had to dress in special clothing and a mask so as not to bring in any bacteria that might be a detriment to his situation. Finally, he left the hospital, and the specialist decided he should have Hyperbaric Treatments. He had to lie down in a unit that actually looked like a coffin with a glass or plastic window over the upper part of the body, and breathe pure oxygen for about 2 or more hours each time. This was to increase the antibiotic circulation in the bone. He had 25 of those treatments before he started to lose his vision. At this point, they decided he was stable, and so he went back to work. The doctor decided to test the strength in his arm to satisfy the requirements of the City. Although he couldn't straighten his arm out flat, Larry was sure he could handle his job. The City did not, and so they decided to give him a disability retirement. He was only 57 years old and really did not want to retire that young. He has always been a "busy" person and couldn't see just sitting around the house for the rest of his life. He did have a period of depression, and so we invested in a business which we thought he would enjoy. It was a monogram business, and he had to run and maintain the equipment which was "right up his alley". Larry ran the business for about 15 to 16 years until another competitor opened up a much larger monogram shop a few blocks from our place. He offered several more services than we did, and he had enough room to display and sell all types of clothing, which we did not. Our business declined to the point that we closed it. However, Larry joined another organization called "Honey-Do Incorporated". I'm sure you know what that means. I have found enough work around the house here for him for the last number of years. It's amazing how many things need to be rebuilt, remodeled, and repaired.

The best part is he didn't lose his arm, and he's able to use it quite effectively for what he wants to do. The infectious disease specialist did tell us at the time that the Staph infection will always live in Larry's system. According to him you never get rid of it. He told us it stays in the bones and can travel through the body. If Larry's immune system gets down, he can and does break out in one or two sores. We have learned to deal with this over the years. We have to offer up our thanks to the Lord for all the progress he's made with that arm.

Several years ago Larry had a TIA (what I call a mini-stroke). He didn't realize what happened to him but told me about it when he got home from work. At that time he was driving a vehicle delivering product to customers. He said as he got back to the small truck, he felt very "funny" and his head hurt. But what really was scary was the fact that he had double vision. He said he looked at a car parked in front of him but saw one car on top of the other. So to be able to drive, he put a tissue over his right eye and held it there with his sunglasses. He said he drove just fine with that eye covered. By the time he got back to the shop, his vision had cleared. When he came home and told me about it I got very worried. I insisted he see our doctor who sent him for an MRI which showed he had suffered a TIA. He never suffered any further ill effects however.

Now to get to the present time. Several months ago I got the feeling that I should clear out some boxes. For the last 8-10 years I have been interested in reading medical newsletters and research. I subscribe to several medical newsletters and had acquired quite a few boxes. I stacked them all close to me and sat in the den with this pile of boxes in front of me. I reached for one of the boxes and found, to my utter delight, a newsletter I had received from a particular doctor written approximately 6 years previous. On the front page was a description of an experimental drug that had been developed to reduce by as much as 80% the effects of a stroke. It had to be administered within two hours of having suffered the stroke. The drug was under investigation at that time but it didn't appear to have any side effects. It was decided this was probably due to the fact that Caffeinol is primarily a combination of caffeine and alcohol. A study showed that neither component on its own had the ability to limit the damage from a stroke, but in combination they worked very well. Based on the content and dosages of the drug, similar protection could be achieved by consuming two or three cups of strong coffee containing Irish Whiskey. If you wanted this type of drink you can go to a restaurant or bar and order an Irish Coffee. The newsletter gave the formula for the Irish Coffee as served in a restaurant or bar. The doctor, however, gave directions so you could make it at home in the event of a stroke. It could work in your favor. He recommended you make <u>2 cups of</u> <u>very strong black</u> <u>coffee to which you add 2 oz. of Irish whiskey</u>. You do not add the sugar or whipped cream as done in a restaurant or bar. An 80% reduction of stroke damage sounded miraculous to me. I thought I had put that newsletter somewhere I could easily find it. However, having found it again at that time turned out to be nothing less than miraculous. I say this because approximately ½ hour later Larry walked into the den holding his head and complaining of "feeling funny", said his head hurt, and when he looked up at me he told me he was experiencing double vision. I remembered immediately his previous TIA a few years back. I sat him down in a chair and checked the directions on the newsletter and went to make him his "Irish Coffee". He drank down the two cups and sat back in the chair to relax. Within about 15 to 20 minutes he said he felt much better and his vision had cleared. He got up and went to work on his computer for the rest of the day. Never did suffer any consequences at all. I asked him if he wanted to go to the hospital to check it out to be sure and he refused. He said he felt just fine. Now – don't you think it was just a bit fortuitous that I picked that day to check through those boxes just ½ hour before he suffered that TIA. I think it was divine intervention, don't you? Thank you again Lord! What a friend we have in Jesus.

Please be careful if you try this formula yourself, I don't know if it would work for every occasion of someone having a TIA or a major stroke. I only know it worked for Larry, I can't make any guarantees for anyone else nor can the writer/ doctor of that newsletter. Better head for the hospital if you are having a TIA or stroke. They will administer the shot there and remember, an 80% reduction in stroke damage is better than no percentage at all. There's no way for you to judge the severity of the situation, that's for the doctors at the hospital to determine. I pray you never have to find out how well that shot works.

SNAP, CRACKLE, AND POP

One of the last years that we lived in Michigan, we decided to take our vacation by staying in a cabin on one of the many beautiful lakes in the state. We rented a cabin and invited my sister, Sharon who was 12 at the time to come with us to keep an eye on the boys who were 4 and 6-1/2. Shortly after we arrived, we noticed the cabin next to ours was rented as well. The couple had a son with them who was approximately the same age as my sister. One beautiful day Sharon asked me if she and the boys could go out in the boat with the young man from next door who had a boat with an outboard motor. They left in the early afternoon and were soon out of sight. The young man seemed to know how to handle a boat so I didn't worry about it too much. It was a very beautiful sunny day.

After they left, I went to sit out in the screened-in porch which faced the lake. I sat close to the screen door in a very comfortable lounge chair. Within about a half hour after the kids left, the weather took a drastic turn, as it can on the lakes, and a storm came up quickly. The waves began to become high with white caps. In Michigan on the lake, that is very dangerous. I started to worry as I couldn't see the kids in the boat. Larry came out to where I was sitting and said he'd better take a boat and go look for them. He left quickly and was soon out of sight. Then I really began to worry with all of them out on that churning lake. As I was sitting looking anxiously at the lake, lightning struck the small evergreen tree right next to where I was sitting in the porch. It snapped in half and fell to the ground. The bolt of lightning was so loud that I couldn't hear for about a 1/2 hour. However, I was concentrating more on the boats than the lightning. Soon I could see two boats coming into shore. They tied the boats to the dock and all came into the screened-in porch. I was so happy to see everyone safe I forgot I couldn't hear anything. I thanked the Lord for bringing everyone back safely. I really was concerned about the incident not turning out as well as it did. I'm sure the young man's parents were just as grateful. My hearing slowly returned to normal, which took about another 1/2 hour. When I could hear better, they told me all the exciting details of the boat ride. To them it was quite the experience. As for me, I made up my mind they would never go out in a boat by themselves again.

As far as myself and the lightning is concerned, I'm glad I wasn't standing outside of the porch next to that tree or I may not be here either. Thank you again Lord for looking out for all of us!

ACCIDENTS, ACCIDENTS

N o one wants to get involved in car accidents, including me. However, that is not how life works. I was 12 years old when I was a passenger in my cousin's car. Our family had gone up to Northern Michigan as my Dad was involved in a Drum and Bugle Group, and the whole family went up to see the Competition. My Aunt and my cousin asked me if I wanted to ride home with them after the Competition was over, and I thought that was a fine idea. I was sitting in the backseat when all of a sudden I got an urge to lean forward and say something to my Aunt who was in the front passenger seat. There were no seat belts in cars 60 years ago so it was no problem to lean forward. I put both my arms on the back of the front seat and was just about to speak when my cousin said " Oh my" !. He never got to finish the sentence as there was a loud crash as we were hit from behind and pushed part way off the road. I should mention that we were on a country-type road with no curbs and just dirt on either side. The car that hit us came to a stop about 50 to 75 feet or more down the road. They hit us so hard that their front bumper was resting on the ground. It was determined by the police that they hadn't even applied the brakes as there were no skid marks. They were deer hunters (as it was deer hunting season in Michigan) and were very inebriated. They hit the back of the car so hard that the trunk was pushed almost to the back seat. The back seat where I had been sitting before leaning forward was split in two. The police officer asked me if I was o.k. He told me had I been resting back in the seat I probably would have a broken back and perhaps a broken neck. I can't even remember what it was that I wanted to ask my Aunt, but at this point it really doesn't matter. I just wonder about the urge to ask her a question at just the right time. Hmmmmmmmm, interesting!

The next accident was two weeks later. I was a passenger in my older sister's car. She had a bench seat in the front and I was sitting in the middle. We were going along at a pretty good rate of speed when she looked away from driving to say something to her friend who was also sitting in the front seat next to the door. Unfortunately, the car in front of her stopped but she didn't. We hit that car at full speed. Both my knees hit the knobs on the radio and that hurt. I think my right hand hit the dashboard as it hurt as well. Moral of the story - don't take your eyes off the road when you are driving!

Accident #3 was related to Larry driving and my telling him to stop as we were going to get in an accident. You will read about that in one of the pages further in the book.

Accident #4 – was just a minor one. We had been out on a date and were on our way back to my house. It was late and I was very tired. I was sitting in the front seat with Larry but decided I needed to rest before we got to my house. It would take about another 1/2 hour so I laid my head on his lap. Shortly thereafter, he either side swiped a car that was parked at the curb or hit the curb itself. I believe he was tired and fell asleep while driving. At least no one was hurt.

Accident #5 – This was another fender bender. My sister was backing out of a parking spot at the local store, I was a passenger in the front seat. She backed up too fast and hit the car parked in back of her which threw us both in a forward motion. I believe I hurt my neck on that one also as we both were more or less thrown forward.

Accident #6 - Larry and I had a VW bus which we both really enjoyed driving. We were on our way for a drive out to the desert. By this time of course, seat belts were required. We were talking and suddenly Larry dropped something on the floor. I unbuckled my seat belt to retrieve it. Larry looked down and again, the cars in front of us stopped but we didn't. Fortunately I was bending forward to retrieve whatever it was that had fallen on the floor. When Larry hit the car in front of us I just kept going from the momentum and fell under the front dashboard. My head hit the underside of the dashboard which didn't feel very good but at least it wasn't more serious.

Now you are probably wondering if I have any ill effects from these accidents. I can tell you that I do. I have 3 degenerating discs in my lower back, and 3 in my neck which hurt a great deal of the time. I have been to therapy, chiropractors, specialists and had acupuncture treatments. They all help but if I overdo my back and neck they let me know. I can't lift my right arm over my head as my shoulder snaps out of place. (That's when I hurt my arm in the accident with Larry). When I bring my arm back down to my side my shoulder snaps back into place. It is a rather painful exercise so I don't often lift my arm in that manner.

I can tell you one thing, I am almost petrified to ride in a car with someone else driving. I do all the driving in our family, I feel better that way! Also, I try to pay attention to what God is telling me. Sometimes it's just a feeling that I should take a different route than I usually take or something similar to that. I truly believe He has kept me safe these last number of years.

BABIES / BABY

In late summer of 1957 I didn't feel very well and didn't know why. I was having all sorts of female problems but didn't go to the doctor's. Finally, when I had a very definite hemorrhage I confided in my older sister, and she quite naturally advised me to see her specialist. She thought I might have a tumor which, of course, scared me as well. After the examination, the doctor looked me in the eye and said "you know what's wrong with you don't you?" I replied, no. He just looked at me and said "you are approximately 3 months pregnant." "It appears you were to have twins but you lost one of them with that hemorrhage, but the other one seems to be all right." "I will give you some pills to stop the bleeding." I wasn't really expecting what he told me but was thankful at least one of the twins was still alive. I had a gnawing feeling though that something would be wrong with the baby as I was having so much trouble carrying him/her right from the start. The doctor told me to come back to see him in two weeks. I didn't want to go back to him as he was so distant from my house, and the hospital to which I would be delivered was quite a distance as well. I spoke with my best friend about that and she suggested I go see her doctor. He wasn't a specialist but he had delivered her babies, and she thought he was very attentive. I agreed and went to see him and she was right, I liked him right away. As I progressed in the pregnancy I didn't seem to be gaining any weight. I only gained 12 pounds the entire balance of the 6 months. I didn't wear maternity clothes until the last 2 weeks before our son was born. The doctor warned me the baby would probably only weigh about 3 pounds which worried me as well. The most serious thing was the fact that I have RH negative blood and Larry has RH positive. The doctor explained to us that was very serious. If the baby was born with RH positive blood there was nothing to do at that time except to change the baby's blood or else he/she would die. He asked me to call him when I felt the labor pains so he would have time to call the hospital to have the blood warmed. Blood is kept under refrigeration and has to be heated in order to transfuse. It was not a pleasant pregnancy but then when are they ever.

I had quite a few labor pains the last month before Patrick was born. The doctor could only give me an educated guess as to a delivery date because of all the earlier bleeding. He said it would be sometime in March. The interesting thing was that I gained most of those 12 pounds the last 2 weeks before Patrick was born. The "big" day finally arrived. I had to call Larry home from work as he worked the afternoon shift, and my pains came on strong about 6:30 pm. Since we didn't know when the baby would arrive, I had gone to work that day. When he arrived home we went to the hospital as planned and Patrick was born at 3:25 am. I had a cold and naturally he was born with one as well. He was put in an incubator for two days as the skin around his mouth and nails was blue. The doctor came and told me that they didn't have to change his blood as it was not necessary. I was very thankful for that. Also, amazingly enough he weighed in at 7 lbs.

The interesting or unbelievable part of this story follows: When I was in the labor room I wondered why I saw very little of my doctor. Upon entering the delivery room, I was asked if I wanted to be put to sleep and I replied that I did. When I delivered Patrick, I assumed the doctor had been in attendance the whole time as I had been anesthetized and had no way of knowing anything different. I didn't find out what really happened that early morning in the delivery room until about a month later. My Aunt and Uncle knew the doctor and his wife. Both couples belonged to a card club and had known each other for years. My Aunt told me she and my Uncle played cards with the Doctor and his wife a few nights after the delivery. The doctor explained what really happened that night. He told them he kept running in and out of the room because he had another patient who was delivering a baby about 20 minutes behind me. When Patrick was born they tested his blood and found his blood was compatible, and presented no problem. However, the doctor's other patient had a 10 pound baby who unexpectedly was born with Yellow Jaundice so severe he would have died except for what happened next. The doctor was able to use the blood that was meant for Patrick to save that baby's life by totally transfusing his blood. The doctor was very stressed. He told everyone he wrestled with the thought that he would have had to let the other baby die if Patrick had needed that blood. There would not have been enough time to warm blood for the other baby. In other words, he would have had to make a life and death decision. One baby lives, one baby dies. It was just too much of a decision, and he was most grateful that it worked out the way it did.

Don't you think it's amazing how God plans things. My baby was spared being aborted with his twin in the beginning, and was born just before the other baby who needed the blood that had been prepared for my baby. It's beyond being a coincidence, don't you think? So both of these children were born, grew up to be handsome young men and believers in the power of the Lord (we hope). No, we don't know who the other child was nor did my doctor ever tell me about this incident. If my aunt and uncle hadn't known him, we would never have found out what really happened that night. Occasionally during family gatherings Patrick says he wonders what has happened to the other baby. We can only hope that he grew up and is well, and understands that God spared his life that fateful night. We're grateful that it turned out as it did, and our Patrick is well aware how God plans things long before we even know they are going to happen. I say this because my friend who sent me to her doctor and I have known each other since grade school. We went to the same parochial high school and remained friends after graduation. Had we not remained friends, I would never have consulted her and gone to her doctor, and most likely that baby would have died. Yes, God plans things long before we are even aware of them. Thank you again, Lord!

STALKED

Shortly before Larry and I got married he acquired a position at one of the Big 3 automobile technical centers. Unfortunately, it was on the afternoon shift which meant he worked from 4:00 pm to 12:30 am. He usually arrived home at 1:00 am. It wasn't easy to get used to but it was a good job with a good future. As time passed, the children came along and I mentally adjusted to being alone every evening except on Saturday and Sunday. I worked during the day and Larry worked during the evenings. One summer night I had put the children to bed and was watching television. It was a Friday night so I stayed up later than usual as I didn't have to get up to go to work the next day. Around 11:00 pm the front doorbell rang. It made my heart beat a little faster as I wasn't expecting anyone, especially at 11:00 pm. I went to the front door and looked through the small window in the door. There was a young man standing on the porch looking back at me. I asked him what he wanted, and he asked for directions to some street with which I was not familiar and so I told him this. I went back to sit down in the den and then heard our standard Poodle in the basement stairwell barking like crazy. I opened the basement door and saw the door handle being turned (fortunately the door was locked), and heard this young man telling the dog to "shut up". He kept turning the door handle in vain, the door was locked. Eventually he gave up and left. I was very frightened. I called my sister who lived a short distance away and she told me to call the police.

Two officers drove up approximately 45 minutes later. They came in the house and I relayed the circumstances to them. They looked at me and made mention of the shorts I was wearing (it was summer), and what did I expect going around dressed like that. I told them to turn around and look at the drapes that were drawn and had been all evening. I always close all drapes when it starts getting dark no matter where I live. I believe this is because of the man who tried to kill me and then peeked in our windows for years. They went outside and looked around. Soon they came back in and said they couldn't find any footprints leading to the side door. I told them that wasn't unusual as we had a totally cement driveway and walk leading to the side door. It hadn't been raining so naturally there couldn't have been any footprints. They asked me if I was "having that time of the month" as women get "funny" at that time of the month and imagine things. I was totally insulted. They left after telling me they would put in the report at the office. I thanked them for coming and left it at that.

About 2 months later I got a phone call one evening from a detective at the police station. He told me they had caught the prowler who had been in our neighborhood. It seems this was a 15 year old boy who lived several blocks down the street. Every Friday night his parents would drive him to the main street on which there was a movie theater. He always told them he would walk home after the show. What he did in fact was peek in windows all the way home. He told the police that he figured by that time of night he would be able to catch some woman in her night clothes as he was peeking in the windows. It was not explained to me how they caught him. I was happy they had and I thought that was the end of it. Unfortunately, it was only the beginning. Several months went by and I stopped at the corner drug store on my way home from shopping. I pulled into a parking spot, cut the engine and turned to open the door. I looked up and saw that young man standing next to the door waiting for me to get out. I really didn't know what to do. I thought I would just get out of the car and ignore him. As I opened the door, he stepped back to let me get out. As I turned to lock the car door, he grabbed my arm from behind. I swung around and he let go of me and then slapped me on my behind when I turned back to lock the car door. I told him to get away from me or I would call the police again, he just laughed. When I got home I was really shaking and told Larry what had happened, he immediately called the police. They came out but weren't too happy about it. However, they did relay an interesting piece of information to us. It seems the Police Captain and this young man's father were long-time friends so they weren't happy to be receiving calls about this young man. The next day my phone rang shortly after I got home from work. The lady identified herself as the young man's Mother. She informed me that her son knew my husband worked nights and I was by myself, and that I had two small children. She told me to keep a careful watch on my children as "something might happen to them". I told her to take her son to the doctor as he had a problem. She just laughed and said he was "just curious, it meant nothing". Unfortunately the high school this young man attended was down the street a short distance from our house. Every day he had to pass our house to get to school. He would stand in front of our house out on the street and just stare at the house. I made sure the children were never in the front yard, ever. Soon the phone calls started, usually in the evening or during the day and evening on the weekends. When I would answer I could just hear heavy breathing on the other end. I would hang up. Sometimes Larry was home to answer the phone and the caller would hang up. The interesting thing to know at this point is that we had always had an unlisted number. I can only imagine how he got our phone number. There were no computers at that time to easily look up numbers as you can do today. We are talking about 49 years ago. You probably are wondering why we didn't change our phone number. Larry and I discussed that but also reasoned out that due to the friendship between the Police Captain and the boy's father, it would not be difficult for the father or the son to be able to get our new number, so we left the number stand.

One weekday evening my doorbell rang. I had the front door open as it was summer but the screen door was locked. I was looking at a gentleman I did not recognize. I glanced at the driveway in which his car was parked and saw the young man in the front seat. The man told me he wanted to bring his son in and get this straightened out. I told him only if he could wait for the police to come and be a part of the meeting. He grabbed the screen door handle and gave a good enough jerk that he broke the lock. He came in the house and walked toward me in a threatening manner, and I could tell he had been drinking. I started to walk backwards as he came toward me, and as he approached me he pushed me down on the sofa. I thought he was going to kill me, and I was very concerned about my two boys who were playing in their bedroom in the back of the house. He warned me once again about his son knowing I was by myself every evening, and about the two young children. He said he didn't know why his son was interested in me especially since I was married and had two children. He told me to stop enticing his son, to leave him alone. I told him to please tell his son to leave me alone! He finally left, got in his car and drove away. I thought of calling the police but remembering what I was told about he and the Captain, it seemed useless. The mother called me shortly thereafter and repeated the threat once again. The phone calls and watching the house went on for almost 4 more years.

A few blocks up the street we had a small shopping center where we did our grocery shopping. Many times I would come out of the store and see this young man on his bicycle at the far end by the driveway. I would hurriedly get in my car and drive out of that parking lot as fast as I could. I would look in my rear view mirror and I could see him pedaling as fast as he could toward me. As soon as I got to the other driveway and onto the street, he would stop and turn around and go back to the entrance driveway on his bike, and wait. I just assumed he was looking for me, little did I know. Near the end of those 4 years I was at the grocery store one day on my way home from work. When I got up to the checker, I could hear all of these excited, nervous conversations back and forth between the checkers about some young man. I asked why everyone seemed so upset. She told me a story that made my blood run cold. It seemed as though this young man would wait by the driveway of the Center on his bike. When he would see a female, alone, go into or come out of the store by herself he would ride up to her on his bike and expose himself. As she was screaming and in shock, he would turn his bike around and get out of there fast. He only lived a few blocks away so by the time the police came he was long gone. This had been going on for some time. Of course, no one knew he lived just a few blocks away. The day that I went to the store the same incident happened to a lady who was just going into the store. She just looked at him and said "big deal" when he exposed himself to her. Evidently he thought he hadn't made much of an impression on her, and never imagined she would do something about it once she got into the store. What he didn't know was that when she got inside, she told the Manager who called the police. They arrived as he was dragging a 9 year old girl around to the back of the market in the alley. Obviously they arrested him, and truthfully I don't know what happened to him after that. I can only say it was such a relief to me, and I thank the Good Lord for keeping my children and myself safe from him for those 4 years. I'm sure the Mother of that little girl was thankful as well. I wish that boy's Mother had taken her son to a doctor when I originally asked her to do that. If she had, maybe someone would have been able to help him before all of this happened. I thank God for His watchful eye over my children, myself, and that little girl.

OUCH, THAT HURT!

W e moved to California from Michigan when the boys were 5 and 7-1/2. We shipped our car on the train and all of us came out on the Super Chief. We brought our standard Poodle with us on the train. We had a compartment and the dog was able to stay with us. It was one of the last years the Super Chief ran, and we were and are very happy we were able to experience the trip in that manner. We lived for a time in apartments then decided that we needed a home for the kids. We purchased a home in Orange County which was not as well populated as Los Angeles. There was only one traffic light in town, and the train ran down the main street to a packing plant a few blocks from our house to unload oranges, lemons and such. There was only one small, and I do mean small, shopping center in town. Most of the property on what is now our main streets was orange groves, lemon and avocado trees, and very small agricultural farms. There weren't that many homes and neighborhoods then but obviously times have changed. When our boys were growing up and got into their teens, they seemed to always have something they wanted or needed. The usual things such as a bike, clothing and such items were understandable, but when they started wanting new stereo equipment, etc. we told them they would have to earn the money to buy those "extras" for themselves. It was still a time when young teenagers could deliver papers, pump gas or cut lawns for extra money.

Patrick decided he wanted a new stereo with big speakers and earphones so he could lie in bed and listen to the music, he was 14 at the time. He got a part-time job after school pumping gas at the local gas station. He soon saved enough to buy his stereo equipment and big speakers. We brought the new equipment home, and he decided one of each of the 4 speakers should go in each corner of his bedroom. His bed was pushed up to the corner of the room, and he wanted one speaker in the corner over his bed. He and his Dad put the speakers up. The speakers were quite big with a wooden case. I must admit he did enjoy the music and using his earphones. One night, very late, we heard a big bang which woke us up. As we ran into Patrick's bedroom, Larry flipped on the light and we found Patrick sitting on the floor. He looked up at me and asked why I had pushed him out of bed. I couldn't understand what he was talking about and told him so. Then we all looked at his bed and were speechless. The big speaker that had been positioned near the ceiling right over his bed was now deep into his pillow right where his head had lain. Evidently whatever was used to hold the speaker in place had broken, and the speaker had fallen into his pillow. I questioned him about the pushing out of bed. He said he had been sound asleep, and someone literally pushed him out of bed onto the floor where we found him when coming into the room.

Who pushed him out of bed you ask, we don't know. What we do know is that it wasn't one of us. But Someone did, and surely Someone saved his life that night, or at least saved him from some very serious injury. Thank you again, Lord!

THAT WAS SOME SIDE ACHE

I had a most unusual thing happen to me when I was 30. I have always had side aches pretty much as long as I could remember before that time. My Mom never really paid much attention to them when I was a child. My grandparents emigrated from Poland and leaned heavily on herbs and remedies handed down through the family, and my Mom usually followed the same procedure. We never even had aspirin in the house while I was growing up. If you had a pain you just toughed-it-out until it eventually went away. We did have to acquire the services of a doctor when I was 5 as our school required a physical and a "school shot" in order to enroll. When I received that "school shot" from the Doctor I almost passed out, and it was necessary for the Doctor to carry me back to the examining room. As I was relating this information to my present family doctor, he asked me what kind of a shot it was. I didn't know as it was just called the "school shot". My present doctor told me if I had that shot again for any reason, I would die before they could do anything. It was obvious I was allergic to whatever was in that shot.

But getting back to my terrible side ache, it was so tremendous that I did go to a doctor we found in our area when we moved to California from Michigan. He was a very busy physician but personable. After he poked and pushed on my right side, he told me it was nothing about which to be concerned as a cyst broke on my ovary on that side. He gave me some pain pills and told me to go home to bed until I felt better. I could barely drive the car, but I headed for home and my bed. I took the pain pills and stayed pretty much in bed for about a week. Slowly the pain subsided and I began to feel better. Now lets fast-forward 4 years.

I always seemed to have so many female problems, and it got so serious my Obstetrician finally decided I should have a hysterectomy. Personally, I was hoping this would solve my female problems, and was assured that it would. The surgery was scheduled for July 2nd, and my doctor told me he would be leaving directly after the surgery as he and his family were going on vacation to Hawaii. The surgery was performed, and I awoke the next day feeling very groggy. Soon after awakening, a doctor came up to my bed and asked how I was feeling. He explained he was the Anesthesiologist for my operation. He asked me if my doctor had been in to see me, and I told him of his vacation plans. He then said "well, I'm going to tell you what happened." He held out his hand and said he wanted to shake my hand as that I was lucky to be alive. My first thought was I had cancer and would have died without the surgery. He went on to tell me of the surgery. He said when my surgeon "opened me up" they saw that my uterus was about the size of a very large cantaloupe. According to state law they had to perform a pregnancy test which turned out negative as he had expected. The Pathologist was called in and he cut the uterus in half, and the entire inside was one big tumor. Fortunately, it turned out to be benign as were all the tumors in my right ovary and tube he removed. He also told me had the tumor in my uterus been allowed to continue to grow, it would have eventually burst and killed me. I breathed a sigh of relief. He said wait, that's not the big news. He went on to ask me if I had a very bad side ache approximately 4 years previous. I replied that I had. He asked me if I had gone to the doctor and I said I had. He asked what was the outcome of that visit, and I told him about the cyst that had broken on my ovary. He looked at me quite seriously and said, that was no cyst, your appendix had burst. He asked me if I knew how long the appendix was and I replied I did not.

He explained the appendix is about as long as your little finger. It had burst and sealed itself twice and grown approximately 8 to 10 inches long and about 2+ inches in diameter. He said there were 2 one inch scars which meant that the appendix burst twice and then sealed again. It wound around my gall bladder, and grew to the point to contain all of the poison. I had been walking around like that for 4 years. He told me it was unheard of, and that every doctor who was in the hospital that day came into the operating room to see this phenomenon. He told me I would probably be in some medical book some day. Not one of the doctors had ever seen such a thing, and were astonished I hadn't died initially when it burst.

So what do you think, would you call that an act of God or just luck. Well, I don't believe in luck, God has a plan for my life and dying at that time was not part of His plan for me. Thank you again, Lord.

During the next nine months, the pains in my stomach became worse and more unbearable. The doctor had not removed the left tube and ovary during the first surgery, so a second surgery nine months later was planned. The surgery was performed and went smoothly. All adhesions were also removed and a special cross stitch was used to discourage any further adhesions from forming. A Urologist had been called in before the surgery as it was discovered through testing that the remaining ovary had grown so large it was resting on my bladder and had almost rubbed a hole through it. The Urologist had to literally fold and sew a flap over the area that would permanently remain that way. The night before I was to go home after the surgery I was not feeling very well. About 11:00 pm I rang my buzzer for the nurse. An older lady came into the room to answer the buzzer, and she was very concerned about my pain, and said she would go get me some pain pills. In a very short time she returned and asked me to hold out my hand. When I did this she put 6 pills in my palm and handed me a glass of water. I took all the pills as she directed. Within a short period of time I fell asleep. The next morning no one could wake me up. Finally, two nurses literally picked me up out of the bed, stood me up on the floor and sat me in a chair near the bed. I could barely keep awake, and I started to fall out of the chair. One nurse held me in the chair and the other made up the bed. After this was done, they both assisted me back to the bed.

I lay there for about ½ hour, and then a nurse came in and scolded me for not getting dressed as I was supposed to be going home that morning. Larry was coming to pick me up shortly. When Larry arrived, the nurse brought a wheelchair into the room and told me to get out of bed and into the seat. I couldn't move very well so she helped me into the chair, and I promptly almost fell out onto the floor. She was very upset with me for being so sleepy, and I began to cry. I tried to tell her about the 6 pills but she said that wasn't true, I was just excited to be going home. At this same time, a doctor passing my room wondered what all the fuss was about and came into the room. He took one look at me and told the nurses to put me back in bed, and I was to stay there. He told Larry that I wouldn't be allowed to go home until the next day, so Larry left to go back home.

After everyone left I fell into a half asleep again. But not like any sleep you would imagine. With my eyes closed or open, I began to see huge purple and green shapes like giant balloons come out of the wall across from my bed. They floated in the air and then came at me and passed through my body into the wall behind the bed. Then I began to float upward, approximately about 1-1/2 feet above the bed. I remember waving my hands below my body to feel where was the bed. Suddenly my feet separated from my legs at the ankles and drifted toward the wall across from my bed and went through the wall. I got very upset as I wondered how I was going to walk again without any feet. This went on for a period of time, I just don't know how long. Eventually I fell asleep and did not wake up until dinner time when the trays were brought in. When I finally did awaken the lady in the next bed said to me, "well, you've had quite a day"! I asked her what she meant, and she told me I was saying all sorts of crazy things about feet floating, giant balloons, and waving my arms around saying something about where was the bed. I told her what had happened to me during that time and I didn't know why. She looked at me and said, "I do." I looked questioningly at her and she proceeded to explain. She told me that after I took the pills the night before, I fell asleep very quickly. About ½ hour later she began to have stomach pains and rang for the same night nurse. When the nurse came into the room, my room mate told her she had pains and would like something for the pain. The night nurse commiserated with her but told her she had already been given her pills, and was not able to be given anymore. So my room mate reasoned that I had been given my pills and her pills which accounted for the total of 6. Larry came to pick me up the next day and

I was much better. When my doctor returned from vacation and I had to go for my checkup I tried to tell him what happened, but he looked at me quietly and didn't say a word. I can say honestly with all my heart, I am now extremely cautious about taking any drugs even if prescribed by my doctor.

Thank you Lord for getting me through that – I couldn't have done it without You!

A short while after the surgery, my Obstetrician decided I needed hormone pills to eliminate the hot flashes etc. I took these pills for quite a few years. At one point I noticed a problem with my right breast, and went to see another doctor as my previous doctor had passed away. The new doctor told me I needed a Ductogram to determine the extent of the problem, and so that was performed. It was discovered that I had many tumors in duct #7 and it would have to be removed. Once again I was concerned about cancer. The surgery went just fine, and I was back to work in a few days. A week later I went to the doctor for a checkup. Before the doctor came into the room, the nurse told me there were many tumors but all were non-malignant. I just shook my head in relief. She looked at me rather curiously and said, "but you already knew that didn't you". I nodded my head, yes. I had counted on the Lord's help once again.

LIKE MOTHER LIKE SON

Patrick had an experience with his appendix that was somewhat similar to mine.

When he was about 18 or 19 I remember his telling me his side hurt, so I suggested we go to the doctor's to check it out. But as most kids of that age, they never seem to want to do what's practical or obvious, so we didn't call for an appointment as he refused to go. Finally, one day about two weeks after telling me about his side, he went to see our family doctor on his own, I was not aware that he went. As the doctor was examining him Patrick was relating how his side hurt and how much it hurt. He took note of the protrusion on his right side. Our doctor, who is a great diagnostician, told him that he was one fortunate individual. He said that somehow tissue completely surrounded his appendix before it burst and kept all the poison contained within a sack which had formed around the appendix. Our doctor told him the body was an amazing thing.

He did have a lump which protruded out of his right side but eventually that too subsided. We don't know if the sack is still surrounding the appendix as Patrick has never had any surgery which would verify the sack is still there. We thank the Lord his appendix did not burst before the sack formed and cause a great deal of trouble, or even death.

Amazing as it may seem, as far as I know Patrick has not had any further problems with his appendix, and he is now in his 50's. Don't you wonder how on earth tissue could grow to form a sack complete enough to surround the appendix and contain all the poison?

We know Who to thank for that, don't we!

HARD TO BREATHE

When Patrick was in his early 20's he and his girl-friend went skiing in the mountains not far from our home. It can be absolutely beautiful weather at the lower elevations, but the mountains can also be very beautiful in the winter when it snows at the higher elevations. The two of them decided to take a day trip to the mountains to ski. We had given Patrick skiing lessons for Christmas that year and he was ready to "hit the slopes". During one of the runs down the mountain, he hit a huge rock which was not visible as it was covered with snow. He fell on top of it which caused him a great deal of pain. However, he got up and continued skiing down the mountain. When he go home that night he told me what happened. I told him to keep an eye on it as he could have a broken rib or something. At the time, he was working for a tool & die company. He continued to go to work everyday even though he did not feel well, and was dizzy most of the time. About 1-1/2 to 2 weeks later he was driving a fork lift and felt very dizzy and knew he was going to pass out. He started to get down from the fork lift and literally did pass out. He woke up and crawled over to the wall and leaned against it. One of his co-workers found him and told his supervisor who sent him home. He decided it was time to go see our doctor. The doctor asked him what was the problem, and then started to examine him. When he was "thumping" on his back he asked Patrick what that felt like. Patrick replied that it felt like bubbles in his back. The doctor immediately sent him upstairs to get an X-ray. When the doctor looked at the X-ray he was amazed again. He said Patrick had cracked a rib when he fell on the rock, and it had punctured one lung. Fortunately, the puncture had closed and his lung was now filling with air again. The doctor told him had he come to see him earlier, he would have put him in the hospital. Now that the lung was filling with air on its own, he told Patrick to go home and take it easy.

Thank you again Lord for looking out for our Patrick!

Several years ago Patrick was having a great deal of trouble with his back and stomach hurting. One Saturday morning he was not able to go to work. He told his wife that his back and stomach hurt so much he couldn't bend over to tie his shoes. He asked her to take him to the hospital (you have to know this is very unusual for him). Once there, through a complete examination they found that he had only 20% of his liver functioning. They told him that if he had not come in that Saturday, he would have been dead by Monday. For the rest of the day they gave him IV's and flushed out his system. He spent several weeks going to a Specialist who told him it would take some time, possibly years, but the liver would regenerate. He is still very careful of what he eats and drinks. I don't know if his liver is totally regenerated, but he does feel better and we hope for the best. Once again, wasn't it fortuitous that he went to the hospital when he did or a few days later he would have died. That's just too coincidental! Thank you Lord once again for looking out for our Patrick.

UNBELIEVABLE BUT TRUE

L arry's parents only visited us once since we left
Michigan for California. That was unfortunate, however, Larry's Mom came out several times after the passing
of Larry's Dad. Larry was travelling at that point in his career
as a consultant/repair person for a well-known heating and
air conditioning manufacturer. His Mom wondered if she
might come out for a longer visit, and we were happy to
comply. During part of her visit Larry had to go out of town.
I suggested she and I go to Las Vegas for the weekend as
my aunt lived there, and we could stay at her place and "do
the town". We had a great time, but soon it was Sunday and
I had to get back to California for work the next day. It was
pretty much mid-morning when we started our trip back. It
was quite windy at my aunt's house, but I really didn't pay
much attention. As we got closer to downtown proper, it

became quite windy with papers, etc. literally flying around. Las Vegas was not as built-up at that time as it is now, and you soon ran out of buildings and were in the desert shortly after leaving the area of the strip. By the time we went a block or so past that point, the wind picked up unbelievably and I couldn't even see the white stripe on the side of the road, nor the middle stripe, nor the road at all. As a matter of fact, I couldn't see the hood emblem on the car. I drove slowly but steadily onward. My Mother-in law asked if we were going to stop as other cars had done initially when the wind first became forceful. At that time, my car was a small Gremlin and I feared that if I stopped and got off the road into the sand we would be stuck or worse. I responded by telling her I thought we ought to keep going. I asked her to watch out the side window to make sure I was on the road. I could tell she was extremely apprehensive because as she held onto the dashboard, she left her fingernail prints in the material. The wind was blowing what seemed like gale force and swirled around, over and under the car. I had to hold on very tightly to the steering wheel as it seemed like the wind wanted to take us in every direction but on the road. I had never been in a desert sand storm before so didn't really know what to expect. We had made previous trips back and forth between California and Las Vegas so I knew the road was fairly straight with few curves. We drove like that for about 250 or more miles. It seemed to take forever to get those miles behind us, and looking at the clock when we finally reached the upward slope of the road into the mountains, it did in fact take many more hours than it usually took. The wind continued at that force until we started up into the San Bernardino Mountains, then it became quiet and calm. We both breathed a sigh of relief. We continued on driving until we reached our house in Orange County. As we pulled into the driveway and I stopped the car, my Mother-in-law turned around to start getting cases out of the backseat. I told her to forget it and let Larry come out and get our luggage for us, we were both exhausted from that drive. Larry went out to get our luggage and soon came back in the house and asked us to come outside with him. When I turned the corner around the garage, the hood of the car was up and I saw it was devoid of paint as was the entire front of the car. Larry pointed to the radiator and told me he didn't know how the car kept running as the radiator was full of sand. He then shut the hood and looked at me and asked, "Did you drive with your head out of the window". I responded and said how foolish did he think I was, the wind was blowing like crazy. He directed my attention to the windshield - I was astonished, it was totally sand blasted and frosted! I couldn't see through it into the front seat at all. He repeated his question as to how could I see through a sand blasted, frosted windshield to drive? I shook my head and marveled at that as he was right, how could I see to drive. The next day we called our auto club to come to the house with a flatbed truck to take the car to the repair shop to replace the windshield, the radiator, and repaint the car. I never did ask my Mother-in-law if she could see through that windshield, and she never made a comment one way or the other. I think we were both in awe of the whole situation. Since she has passed away, I will never know the answer to that question until I get to Heaven. As far as I am concerned, I think a miracle happened that day, and I say once again, thank you Lord for Your watchful eye over us that day!

WHO NEEDS
HEADLIGHTS TO DRIVE?

L arry and I love to visit the State of Washington. It's a wonderful drive from Southern California, especially along the coast. The mountains are beautiful and picturesque, and the ocean waves are so relaxing. The ocean is a deep blue, and waves roll and toss themselves against the sand and rocks. At certain times of the year you can see whales. If you stop in Northern California in certain places you can view the antics of the playful seals. Oregon has beautiful redwood forests which makes for a cool, calm and peaceful drive. Also, we love to ride the ferry in the Sound in Washington, and visit small towns which welcome all visitors.

On one of our driving trips in Washington we had gone pretty far north. It was getting late and dark already. We had made motel reservations below Seattle in a small town called Puyallup. It had started to rain very heavily and that makes driving a lot more difficult. I was driving and Larry had the map on his lap. He found a short cut through the mountains, and suggested we take it to save time getting back to the motel. I turned onto that route which literally was a mountain road. The rain was quite heavy and the road was winding with no street lights of any kind. Within a few minutes of turning onto this route all my lights went out. I had no headlights, tail lights, or dash lights. Although there were not that many people on this route, I was totally unfamiliar with the road, and I was concerned about someone hitting me in the rear. I tried turning the light switch on the steering column back and forth but the lights remained off. I was really getting worried as the rain was so heavy, and with no street lights I could barely see the road turning and twisting along the mountains. A car passed me going very fast. I decided I would follow his tail lights as they were very visible. He was going about 75 miles an hour, and I had to stay as close behind him as I could so as to not lose sight of his lights. I kept turning my light switch on and off but no lights came on. I started praying out loud, and I mean out loud asking God to help me stay on the road and keep us from getting killed. I prayed that way for approximately 15 or more minutes. There were no towns along this route at this point, so I had little choice but to keep driving fast to follow the car in front of me. After following those tail lights for about 15+ minutes, there appeared some lights ahead which turned out to be a small town. I took the only exit and we found ourselves in a small community. Fortunately, there was a gas station up ahead. I pulled into it and a young man came running out to see what we needed. I rolled down the window and told him my problem with the lights, and asked if there was a mechanic available. He went around to the front of the car and told me to try the switch again. Amazingly enough, the lights went on. He said, everything looks o.k. to me. I thanked him and rolled up the window. He went back inside as it was still raining very heavily. I looked at Larry and he looked at me and I said, " I don't get it". "I turned that switch at least 10 times or more and nothing happened." We just sat there trying to digest the situation, and then I put the car in drive and we went on our way. It was only about another 10 minutes to the end of the route which exited near the town where we planned to spend the night.

Larry told me I probably didn't turn the switch back and forth fully. I can tell you honestly, this was my car, and I drove it every day and night. I certainly knew how to turn the lights on and off. I think God wanted me to ask for His help, and He certainly did it in a dramatic way. Driving at 75 miles an hour in the pouring rain with no lights on a dark twisting mountain road is an experience I don't wish to repeat. Thanks Lord for getting us through that without incidence.

Another interesting driving incident happened on one of our return trips from Northern California. We had been visiting my friend who lived in one of the towns in wine country on the other side of the Golden Gate Bridge. We had stayed quite late visiting and when we crossed over the bridge, I suggested we drive for just a short distance and then stop for the night. I drove approximately 50 more miles and then we decided to find a motel. I pulled into the parking lot and cut the engine as Larry got out to register us for the night. When he got back into the car it wouldn't start. He opened the hood to see if he could do something about the problem. He eventually asked a trucker to push us into a parking space near our motel room. The next morning we got up and got ready to leave. When I got in the car he lifted the hood and hot-wired the car. He explained to me that we were going to go into the nearest town and he would get a new battery which would solve the problem. But - - he told me I was not to shut off or stall the engine under any circumstances as it would not start again. We went into the town and found a car parts shop. I stayed in the car and kept the motor running. Larry bought the new battery but he did not install it at this time because of some problem with the wiring. (In retrospect, I wish he had installed it, problems or no problems with the wiring). We started on our way. Larry warned me not to stall the car or shut off the engine once again. I had approximately 300+ miles to drive to get to our home. I drove the freeway all the way home only slowing down for traffic, but never actually coming to a full stop as I worried about stalling the car. When I saw cars slowing down and almost coming to a stop, I slowed down ahead of time to avoid a problem. Fortunately, I did not have any actual stop signs to agonize over, just slowing traffic. When we arrived at the exit to our town, I timed the light so I wouldn't have to come to a full stop. I timed all the lights the rest of the way home until I pulled into our driveway and shut off the engine. I have to tell you that it's a lot easier to write about it than actually doing it. What an end to a lovely vacation. Can you imagine driving all that way without once stopping the car or stalling the engine. Some things amaze me. I can tell you that I did a lot of silent praying while on that trip home.

I could just imagine having to stop the car suddenly and not be able to start it again. Just think about the traffic jam that would have created on the freeway. Thanks again Lord, for helping me get through that.

One summer a number of years ago Larry and I took a vacation to Oregon . We had done this a number of times, but enjoyed visiting friends and driving back along the Coast of California which is a beautiful drive on Route 1. This time, I told Larry we wouldn't stop as I was in a little bit of a hurry to get home. Route 1 is a slower drive, but well worth it. However, this time I decided we wouldn't stop and watch the waves as we had done many times before. As we were driving and enjoying the view, I suddenly heard a voice in my ear say "Get off the road". I ignored the voice and continued driving. We passed by another exit and the voice said again, "Get off the road". There was one more exit to the beach and I wasn't going to take it, but the voice practically screamed in my head to "Get off the Road" so I took the last exit to the parking lot on the beach. Larry said to me, "I thought you said you weren't going to stop!" I didn't want to tell him about the instructions in my ear so I just said I changed my mind. We got out of the car, put the leashes on the dogs and walked up and down a short section of the beach for about a half hour. Suddenly, I had a feeling that it was o.k. to get back in the car and continue on our way. I told Larry it was time to hit the road. He said, "I think you're nuts, first you don't want to stop and then we stop." "Now we're enjoying the walk and you want to go." However, he shrugged his shoulders, and we got back in the car and started out of the parking lot. A short distance and the road started up a hill and took a curve to the right. As we got around the curve, we had to quickly stop. In front of me was a logging truck which had taken the curve evidently too fast, tipped over on my side of the road with logs strewn all over the place. As we both looked at that scene, I turned to Larry and said "that's why we stopped at the beach". He just looked at me and shook his head. We both knew had we been in that lane when the truck rolled over into it we would have been under that truck, and it would have been disastrous. The accident had evidently happened while we were running the beach as the police had not even arrived yet. We had to wait about 20 minutes until they came and directed traffic around the logs and the truck. As I passed around all of this, I could only thank the Lord for warning me to stop and park the car, and not go any further until the feeling came upon me that it was o.k. to continue. Thank you again, Lord! That was a close call.

FOOD POISONING
IS NO FUN!

We had lived in California for a few years when my Mom had a very bad heart attack. We decided that we should drive back to Michigan to see her. We drove because we didn't know how long we would be there, and so we packed up what we had and rented a U-Haul trailer to take everything back with us. When we left California we drove on the famous Route 66 into Arizona where we stayed the first night out. The next morning we found a small family-type restaurant to have breakfast before we started off for the day. Larry, Patrick and I ordered scrambled eggs and toast. Son Larry had cereal as usual. I will hereafter refer to Son Larry as Larry Paul to differentiate between husband and son. It will be less confusing I think. When we finished eating we all got back in the car to continue on with our journey. Within about 20 minutes I started to feel ill and so did Larry and Patrick. In fact, we felt so ill that I told Larry I couldn't continue on the trip, he had to find us a motel and I needed to go to bed. Larry Paul seemed fine and said so. We quickly found a motel, and we all went to bed except Larry Paul who watched TV most of the day. The rest of us spent the day making trips to the bathroom. At one point, I went to the bathroom and was so sick I fell on the floor and couldn't get up. Larry crawled into the bathroom and quite literally dragged me by my legs back to bed. He helped me up on the bed and fell back into bed himself. Poor Patrick had to fend for himself as I was too sick to help anyone else. I believe Patrick was about 6 or 7 at the time. By evening we all began to feel better, not great, but better. We hadn't eaten all day, but at that point we were still too sick to go out and find some place to eat. Larry discovered there was a small restaurant next to the motel. We gave Larry Paul some money and told him to go get us all some tea and toast and to get himself a hamburger. I had never done anything like that before, and was really apprehensive about giving him money and sending him on an errand such as that. This was unfamiliar territory, and I was concerned about him going by himself. He was about 9 at the time. However, he did just fine and returned with the tea and toast. I think the food helped us feel a little better. We all went to bed right after eating and didn't awaken until the next morning. When we got up we all felt better, still a little unsteady but better. Larry felt pretty good and as he was the driver, that worked out very well. As we drove that day, we compared notes and symptoms. It was decided that we had food poisoning and thought it must have been the scrambled eggs. As Larry Paul had cereal and wasn't sick at all, it seemed logical that it was the eggs. What a start for a long 5 day driving trip.

My next experience with food poisoning was quite a few years later. The kids had grown and were involved in their own lives. Larry and I love to go to Church on Saturday evenings. There is something about it being dark outside, the lights dimmed inside, and the candles flickering in the Church. I get a feeling of being protected somehow, and that I'm on an almost one-to one basis with the Lord. Anyway, we decided to have dinner before we went to Church one Saturday evening and found a restaurant nearby. I ordered fish and chips which came with coleslaw. It was delicious. After we finished, we left for Church which was just a short distance away. During the service it became apparent to me that I had to visit the Ladies Room as I wasn't feeling very well. When I came out I knew I had better go home right now. Fortunately, we were seated in one of the last pews, and so I stood next to the pew in the aisle and motioned for Larry to come out. When he did, we moved to the back of the Church and I told him I was really ill and needed to go home immediately. At home, I went right to bed and stayed there between bathroom visits. I was so sick I couldn't believe it. Larry had to pick me up out of bed and carry me to and from the bathroom. He wanted to take me to the hospital but I was too sick to go. I'm not into calling for an ambulance either. The next day I started to feel better after I took some medication. A few days later we decided to check with the restaurant regarding the coleslaw. They told me it was made with Mayonnaise and was kept on ice but not in the refrigerator. Believe me when I tell you that I don't ever order coleslaw in a restaurant since that incident. I make my own, and it's kept in the refrigerator.

My next and hopefully my last experience with food poisoning occurred on a trip to Seattle. I have a very dear friend who lived in Northern California at that time, and we decided to stop and see her on the way up. We arrived near dinner time and she suggested we go to this very nice restaurant for take out. That seemed like a great idea as we were tired from the drive, and getting comfortable in her dining room and eating take out seemed just fine. I really wasn't terribly hungry so I decided on just a big salad with a roll. The salad was in a salad bar with all of the ingredients on ice. I made myself a big wonderful salad with all the trimmings. I then packed a small container with the dressing. We took our food to her house and settled down to enjoy a relaxing meal and conversation. At this point, I should tell you it had been 104 degrees in her area that day. Within an hour I was very ill and had to go to bed. I spent the next 5 days in bed trying to get over the food poisoning. My friend and Larry had a totally different type of meal and they were not affected. While I was in bed, my friend and Larry went around to see the sights . My friend made arrangements for a neighbor/ friend to look in on me and get me whatever I needed. What a trip that turned out to be. By the end of the 5th day I was feeling fairly decent, not great but decent. Larry and I talked it over and decided to go back to Southern California instead of continuing on to Seattle. So much for that vacation!

Now when I go out to eat I do not order coleslaw or any type of creamy dressing. I think three times is the charm as they say (for food poisoning that is), don't you?

INTROSPECTION

In thinking back over my life I'm amazed at the number of times God has given me a message, mostly a thought or two that runs through my mind. If we're receptive to those little thoughts they can be a life saver. For instance, I remember a time quite a few years ago when Larry worked in Anaheim, I was taking him to work so I could keep the car for errands. He knew all the back streets and side streets to save time, and so we were on one of those back streets. I was a reasonable distance from the corner where there was a light as it was a main thoroughfare. I could see the light was red so I was slowing down to prepare to stop. All of a sudden, I got the feeling that I should stop the car right then, which I did. As I stopped about 6 - 7 car lengths from the corner, Larry asked me why I had stopped. Just as he got the last word out, there was a collision at that corner and one car spun totally out of control. We watched as it spun around and then headed down the street toward us. I couldn't back up as another car had come up behind me. We sat helplessly as the car headed toward us, and we just waited for the head-on collision. Her car was going pretty fast, and I assumed she was totally out of control and couldn't find the brake pedal. Suddenly the car stopped almost bumper to bumper with our car, and we both stared at a young lady in the other car. As she was so close to our car both of us could look through the windshields and see each other clearly. She just sat and stared at us, I'm sure she was in a bit of shock. Larry got out of the car and ran over to her door. She rolled down the window and he asked if she was o.k. She said she was, and then we noticed a man running down the street towards the cars. I assumed he was the one who had hit her on the corner. As the other man approached the lady's car, Larry came back and got in our car. He turned to me and said, "Do you know how close she was to our car"? I knew it was not too much of a distance and said so. He replied , "there was only about 1 to 2 feet between our bumpers. It was a good thing you stopped this far back from the corner or we would have gotten creamed".

Thank you again Lord.

I also remember an instance when Larry and I were on our way to Las Vegas to look in on my Aunt. The traffic was very heavy but at least it was moving. Our freeways here in California can become like parking lots some times. However, this time I was in what we call the fast lane; I don't usually travel in that lane. We were moving along at about 55 to 65 miles per hour when a voice in my head said, get out of this lane now! I immediately moved into the middle lane and all of a sudden the entire freeway came to a stand still. At this time, the car that had been in back of me when I was in the fast lane hit the car that had been in front of me in that lane. If I had not moved over when I was told, that car would have hit me. I'm not sure how much damage was done but at the speed we had been driving, and for everything to come to a sudden stop, I'm sure it was quite an accident. As I had already moved into the middle lane, I continued driving after we came to the stop and in a few seconds the traffic moved forward once more.

Thank you Lord for the warning!

Larry has gotten a few of those "feelings" as well. Several years ago he just felt as though he should go to our cousin's house for some reason. I was at work so he got in the car and drove over there himself, a distance of about 10 miles. Once he reached the house he rang the doorbell, but no one came to the door. He looked in the street and saw our cousin's car so he knew he was home. He kept ringing the bell. After what seemed a long time Chet answered the door but could barely stand. Larry went in and helped him back into bed. He told him that he was going to take him to the hospital right then. Chet didn't object as he was too sick. Larry got him into the car and drove to the Veteran's Hospital in Long Beach which was a little distance from the house. Chet had to have electric shock to his heart as it was just about ready to stop beating. He was in the hospital for almost a week and the Doctor told him if he hadn't gotten to the hospital when he did he would have died. Chet has asked Larry several times what made him come to the house that day. Larry told him he just had a "feeling".

Just recently, Larry had another feeling that he should go to Chet's house. When he arrived Chet was just going up on the roof attempting to repair some shingles. When he saw Larry get out of the car he came down off of the ladder. Larry inspected the rope that Chet was using around his waist, and the way in which he had placed it around the chimney to make sure he wouldn't fall off of the roof. Unfortunately, he hadn't properly placed the rope and eventually it would have given way and he would have fallen off the roof. It's a two story house so the chances are that he would have gotten hurt in some way. Whether seriously or not, it was avoided by Larry going over there because of one of his "feelings". Chet is still amazed about those "feelings".

NEXT TIME I HIRE A TREE REMOVAL SERVICE

We had planted a small tree, at least we were told it was a tree, near the driveway side of the yard close to the street. After a few years it became evident that it wasn't a tree but a bush. It only bloomed once a year but began to spread out which made it difficult to see past it when exiting the driveway into the street. I asked Larry if he would remove it and just plant grass there. One day while I was at work, he decided this was the day to remove the tree. When I came home the bush (tree) was gone but Larry was not doing well with his back. He said he had dug around the roots and then decided to pull the bush out the rest of the way. It was a tug-of-war and the bush won. Larry fell backward on his spine and back, and it was really hurting. After a few days, I suggested he go see our doctor and have an X-ray, which he did. The X-ray showed he had fractured three vertebrae and crushed one. The doctor also suggested Larry have a Cat Scan which also showed he had a 40% blockage in his Aorta artery. That was unexpected. Our doctor sent him to another doctor who told him he would eventually need a bypass. Larry didn't like the sound of that at all. I had been going to the Whitaker Wellness Clinic in Newport Beach, CA for my blood pressure. The Whitaker Wellness Clinic is an alternative medical establishment. We brought the X-rays and Cat Scan to the Clinic and the doctor inspected them thoroughly. He concurred with the diagnosis of the other doctor. But he did suggest Larry undergo treatment called Plaquex Therapy and Chelation Therapy. He started on his therapy treatments almost immediately. He went in twice a week for 30 treatments each. At the end of that time he had another Cat Scan at the same lab where he had gone originally. The second Cat Scan showed there was no blockage. A follow-up Ultra Sound found his arteries were clear of any blockage and no surgery was necessary. Since that time he goes every quarter for a treatment of each therapy to make sure his arteries stay clear.

When he showed our family doctor the last Cat Scan with the clear arteries he could hardly believe it. I'm sure the doctor/tech who processed his first Cat Scan and the last one where his arteries were clear was somewhat shocked. I understand complete surprise was expressed in the lab when a comparison was made with the "before" and "after" Cat Scans.

I'm thankful that we knew of this Clinic and that they were able to help him as they do many other patients with all sorts of devastating problems. Thank you Lord for such a place to be available to everyone, and so close to us here in Southern California.

MENINGIOMA

One Saturday morning several years ago, I was cleaning the kitchen when all of a sudden my legs just gave out and I fell on the floor. Larry came running into the kitchen and picked me up and put me in a chair in the den. I couldn't figure what had happened except my legs got suddenly weak and I just fell. It took a little while but I seemed to be all right. On Monday morning I thought I had better go see my doctor who has been treating our family for over 35 years. During my appointment, I relayed to him what had happened to me over the weekend. He decided I needed to have a few tests, one of which was an MRI on my brain to see if I had experienced a stroke. I also had an EEG and the results were satisfactory. Our doctor sent me to a Neurologist for the MRI. After the test, I went to the Neurologist's office for the results. He looked over the X-ray and was checking different parts of my brain. All of a sudden he said, "what's this"? I got off the table and joined him while we both looked at the X-ray. He showed me a small round object behind my left eye. It was about the size of a pea, and he pointed out to me that it was floating between the back of my left eye and my brain. He said it was a benign Meningioma. He asked me if I had an accident and hit my head at some point in my life. He said it was part of the covering of my brain that had broken away because of an injury.

I recalled a time when I was about 9 or 10 years old. My friends and I decided to have a bike race down our block. We all lined up and started off. I was pedaling my two wheel bike as fast as I could. I couldn't reach the seat as I wasn't tall enough to sit and still reach the pedals, so I just stood up and pedaled without sitting down. I was really moving when suddenly both of my feet slipped off the pedals. I was literally running with the bike. There was so much momentum that I couldn't stop it with my feet, and the next thing I knew I had turned the wheel and ran into the curb. That's the last I remember until I woke up with a friend on each side of me guiding me home. Blood was running down my mouth as I had bitten the bottom lip through and evidently hit my teeth as well. One front tooth was actually bent backwards, and how I hadn't knocked it out is beyond me. I broke my glasses and my nose as well. The doctor said that was more than likely when the injury to the brain occurred. He told me many people go through their entire lives not knowing they have a Meningioma. Isn't that interesting. Be careful if you fall and hit your head.

At first I had an MRI every six months and when it became apparent that the tumor was not growing, the doctor told me to come back once a year. That was 6 years ago and I still have my tumor, but fortunately for me it remains benign and just floats behind my left eye. I am most grateful that it is benign and pray that it stays that way. Oh by the way, neither doctor could ever figure out why I became so weak that I fell on the floor. But if that had not happened, I never would have found out about the tumor, and the ability to be able to do something about it should it become necessary. Another coincidence perhaps? I think not.

Recently my blood pressure has been misbehaving – too high. I've been on medication for years but this time the medication just made me feel ill all the time due to the many side effects. I had gone to a Specialist for my blood pressure, and he suggested a kidney Ultra Sound. The kidneys are fine except I have a Angiomyolipoma in my left kidney.

It is what's called renal sinus fat or to use a more familiar term, it's a tumor. It is also benign for which I thank the Lord once again.

DOGS, DOGS, DOGS

I can't ever remember a time when we didn't have a dog. When I was growing up my Mom always had a dog. Naturally, it follows that Larry and I would have one or more dogs at all times. We have taken dogs on airplanes to go back to Michigan to visit family, and/or put them in day-care wherever we are on vacation. We have adopted animals from people who can no longer care for them or don't want to. It then follows that we had two wonderful adopted dogs. One had been badly abused and so she was a very quiet 'I don't want to get in your way' Cocker Spaniel. I called her Missy. Then we adopted a dog from a Marine who was being shipped somewhere and couldn't take his Cocker, Cody. They got along with each other very well. Missy was approx. 9 years old and Cody was 5-1/2 years old. They never gave us one moment of grief. As time passed each developed health problems, and Missy passed away at 15 and Cody passed away at 12 years old. For about 2 weeks I didn't want another dog. Then one Saturday I woke up and announced to Larry that I wanted to go buy a dog. So we went to the local pet store in the mall, which was unusual, as we usually get our dogs from breeders or other people. I walked in and looked around - animals everywhere. There were some puppies in the window just tumbling all over each other. I bent over and pressed my nose against the window to watch the fun. One puppy broke away from the group and came up to the window and pressed her nose right where my nose was pressed on the outside. She was red and the cutest thing, I knew right away she was THE one. My husband missed his Cocker Spaniel so we also looked for a Cocker that he chose. We went home that day with two dogs. I thought all the way home what I would name her. The red coloring reminded me of Ginger, and so I named her Ginger. Larry named his puppy Lady Freckles cause she had patches of reddish brown on her coat but freckles all over her nose. We were two happy people. Ginger was a very precocious puppy. She could get into more trouble but I loved her to bits. We had the puppies 9 days when Ginger died. I was heart broken, and I do mean heart broken. I cried for days. I know that probably sounds silly to some of you but I **really** love dogs. Soon it became apparent to me that I needed another dog, so back to the same pet store. I looked around at puppies and one of the salespersons came up and asked me if I would like to see any particular puppy. I noticed some really cute ones in a cage and asked to see them. She put up a low circular fence and put about 5 Schnauzer puppies inside. They were running all around and tumbling all over each other. One of the puppies broke away and came over to Larry and untied his shoelaces. I knew right away that was THE puppy for me. We took her home and I named her Duchess. What a puppy she was. I think she was part human and didn't know it. We put up a baby gate in the kitchen doorway to keep the puppies in the kitchen. I couldn't believe it when she came running into the den. I thought the gate had been left open. I picked her up and took her back in the kitchen. The gate was closed as we had left it. I couldn't figure out how she got out. I put her back in the kitchen and she promptly started climbing up the open shelves of the counter until she reached the top and jumped down over the fence. We couldn't believe it. What a character.

In order to keep both the puppies closer to the doggie door in the living room sliding door, we put a fence from the house to the back fence to keep them on one side of the house. Last year we had some company from Nevada and we went out for dinner. We opened the doggie door in the living room knowing the dogs would have to stay on this side of the house. When we got home from dinner, we found Duchess on the other side of the house by the front gate waiting for us to come home. She looked through the wrought iron gate and wagged her little tail as hard as she could. I asked her "How did you get on this side of the house"? No answer, of course, just a wagging tail. We went outside and checked the gate on the new fence we had installed. It was closed. I couldn't imagine her jumping over it as she was a little tubby and there was nothing to climb up on. The next day we went sight-seeing again. Came home to the same thing. We were really puzzled how this dog was getting past that gate in the backyard. So I decided to do a little test. I closed the doggie door in the living room sliding door and put her outside. I went around to the other side of the house and went out the kitchen door. I walked around the house to the backyard. Sure enough, there was Duchess on the right side of the fence. I stood on the other side and called her to come to me. She ran to the doggie door which I had closed previously. She then ran back to the gate and wagged her tail at me. I called her to come to me again. I could hardly believe what happened next. She took her right paw and slide it between the fence and the edge of the gate and pulled the gate open and slipped through. Now you may ask, did you train her to do that, and the answer is no.

When she was a new puppy to us Larry accidentally stepped on her foot. She promptly rolled over on her back, relaxed her back legs so they just hung open and put her front paws on her chest and rolled her head to the side. We both laughed and said "Call 911, call 911, dead dog". To this day, if you accidentally step on her paw she rolls over and does this trick every time. We took her to the pet store and it happened that Larry accidentally stepped on her foot and she went into her routine. A Lady came running over when she heard Larry say "Call 911, dead dog." He had to explain the whole silly routine to her, and she laughed as hard as he did. No, we didn't teach her that either.

The best part of the Duchess story follows -

I had a very elderly aunt who lived in Las Vegas. She was 99 in Sept. 2008. She never had any children and my Uncle passed away years ago. She was basically by herself except for a very lovely lady whose name is Joy. Joy looked in on my aunt and took her to the doctor, shopping, or whatever else was needed. What a blessing Joy has been. We put my aunt in a facility about 9 years ago but she did have a mobile home in North Las Vegas. I kept it for awhile for two reasons. (1) - it made her feel as though she could go home anytime she wanted (what was not the case) and (2) - it gave us a place to stay when we went to Vegas to visit and take care of her financial affairs. Duchess and Lady Freckles were about 2 years old when we took them for the first time. We had decided to sell the mobile home as it had been broken into by kids who trashed the place. It had been sitting there vacant except for the times we came to visit. We came one weekend and disposed of all the furniture and household goods. We took some home and gave some to Joy's church as they housed the homeless, and could use the furniture and household items. We went back on the Memorial Day weekend to prepare the mobile home to sell. It was in great need of cleaning. Before we left for Vegas, we went to the sporting goods store and bought a blow-up bed as we had distributed all of the furniture in the previous visit. We arrived the Thursday before Memorial Day and started right in cleaning. We worked all day and got quite a bit done. After we came back from dinner, we watched a few TV programs on the set we brought with us. Soon our eyes were closing as we had worked very hard that day. We made up the bed on the floor and gratefully sank into it. I fell asleep quickly, but kept waking up because we had left the swamp cooler on and I was cold. The next morning we got up and started again to finish the cleaning. We worked all day. After coming back from dinner, we watched TV and then decided to go to bed. I didn't mind sleeping on the blow-up bed as it's rather comfortable. We turned out the lights and went to sleep. I asked Larry not to turn on the swamp cooler as I had been so cold the night before. We did close all the doors and windows but it was pleasant enough to fall asleep. Sometime in the middle of the night (I think it was the middle of the night) I heard Larry telling Duchess to leave him alone in a rather loud manner. She was putting her nose under his arm and pushing it upward to wake him up. I tried to sit up and fell back on the pillow. I rolled off of the bed onto the floor and tried to get up. I couldn't sit up. Larry crawled around the bed and grabbed me by the leg and literally dragged me back to the bed. He rolled me up onto the bed, and then crawled around on his hands and knees and opened all the doors and windows in the house, and turned on the swamp cooler. He then fell back into bed and we both went to sleep again with all the windows left open and the swamp cooler on. Duchess did not wake us again. In the morning, we both got up and had a terrible headache, nauseous and felt weak all over. Larry went out to the kitchen and soon came back and told me that there was a leak in the kitchen gas stove. Obviously, he turned off the gas. The kids who broke into the house evidently used the stove and left the gas valve part way open without a flame. They also burned a hole in the kitchen floor. If Duchess had not insisted we wake up, we wouldn't have awakened at all, ever. Interestingly enough, initially we hadn't intended to take the dogs with us on this trip. Because we had so much cleaning to do I thought they would be in the way. However, at the last minute I changed my mind and they came with us. Duchess was o.k. in the morning but Lady was terribly tired. We could barely wake her up. So once again, the Lord put all things together for our good.

That event happened several years ago. Last week I was thinking of Ginger and how I wish she hadn't died, I still miss her. But a thought came into my mind and it was this. If Ginger hadn't died we wouldn't have gotten Duchess, and none of us would be alive today. That sort of puts things in perspective, don't you think. Thanks again Lord! You are so good to us!

Another most interesting thing happened with a dog we had many years ago we called Freckles. We bought Freckles as a puppy from a couple who raised Cocker Spaniels. We chose him because he was not only so cute, he was multi-colored (brownish-red and white) with freckles all over his nose. At that time, we had a monogram business in a commercial building on one of the main streets. Larry ran the business and I worked outside the business. Larry took the puppy to work with him every day as we didn't want to leave him alone in the house. Freckles soon became used to people coming in and going out of the shop, and never barked. However, one day three men came into the shop and asked for change for a bill one presented to Larry. Larry became suspicious when one man went back outside and kept looking up and down the walkway. Larry tried to explain to the two men who remained inside that we didn't have a cash register because people gave us checks. Freckles started to bark and growl so loudly no one could hear the other. The dog tried jumping and jumping but he couldn't reach the counter. He tried to climb up on a table we had near the counter. It became evident that no conversations were going to progress at all so the three men left. The next day we heard these men had gone into the shop next door to us and the pizza parlor at the other end of this little shopping center and robbed both places. No one was hurt but it was a very scary thing to happen in broad daylight. Somehow that dog knew these were not "nice guys". We heard they had a weapon but didn't have to use it. I thank God they didn't use it on Larry or our dog. We were especially happy that he was there that day to protect Larry.

Interesting how that dog always behaved around customers who came in and out of our shop every day except that day with those three men. Somehow, Freckles knew they were there for no good. Obviously their intention was to rob Larry as well. Hmmmmmm – makes you wonder about the instincts of animals, doesn't it. Thank you Lord for those instincts.

Freckles was also a dog who didn't know he was a dog. We seem to get a lot of those types. Freckles loved to go 'bye-bye" in the car. If you didn't take him he would crawl under my baby grand piano and growl at us. One day I decided to go to the local Chinese take-out restaurant to get dinner. I took Freckles with me, naturally. I parked near the door to the restaurant, went inside and started to give my take-out order to the waiter. A car horn began to blow and it didn't stop. It went on continuously and was driving everyone in the restaurant nuts. I thought to myself, why would anyone leave some kid in the car by itself. Just then a couple came into the restaurant and they were laughing so hard they could hardly talk. The waiter asked what was the problem. They said there was a dog in a car in the parking lot which was sitting in the driver's seat and honking the horn with his paw. I knew right away who it was. I excused myself and went outside to the car. As soon as Freckles saw me coming he jumped into the passenger seat. I opened the car door and told him "you don't fool me, I know you have been honking the horn." He just looked at me innocently and I could read his face which said, "who me?" I told him "you don't fool me, cut it out!" I went back into the restaurant to continue placing my order. Within a few seconds the horn business started again. I finally cancelled my order and went out to the car and went home. We had scrambled eggs for dinner!

Larry would take Freckles with him wherever he went. One day they were driving down one of our main streets which has an island between the lanes. A couple who were jogging were standing on the island in the middle of the street instead of having gone to the corner and crossing as they should have. Freckles jumped into Larry's lap and started beeping the horn at the couple. They almost fell off the curb.

As Larry passed them they looked at the dog honking the horn at them with his head out of the window. He can get us into some embarrassing situations. Maybe he thought he was a "Police Dog". What a character!

THANK GOODNESS FOR THE HEIMLLICH MANEUVER

One Saturday Larry and I were sitting at our eating counter talking and eating lunch. Something happened to me that I never thought would happen. I guess I tried to swallow and talk at the same time, and the result was that I couldn't cough up the food or swallow it. I started getting panicked when I couldn't accomplish either one. Evidently Larry noticed that I was having a problem and he quickly got out of his chair, pulled me out of my chair and proceeded to use the Heimlich Maneuver. Within a few seconds out flew a piece of food that had been lodged in my throat. I sure was glad he was there and that he knew what to do.

I had an Aunt who only lived to be 27. A very unfortunate accident happened to her when she was 5 years old. She was sitting on the curb in front of their house in the town where they lived in Pennsylvania. A young man came around the corner on a motorcycle, revved up the engine and frightened her terribly. She went into convulsions and was taken to a hospital where she was evidently given too much medication. Sadly, she never progressed past the age of 9 or 10. My Grandmother had to put her in a facility in Michigan as she couldn't properly care for her. I remember that we used to take Grandma to visit her when she was in town. Even as a child I felt very sorry for this adult looking person who acted like a child my age. One day at dinner in the facility where she lived, she started to choke on a piece of meat. The only thing people knew to do at that time was pound a person on the back. Obviously, this does not always work, and sadly she choked to death.

I can be thankful when I was choking Larry was there and knew what to do and how to do it. Another coincidence you say, I think not. Thank you again, Lord.

DON'T TALK TO ME ABOUT ANTIBIOTICS

S everal years ago I got an earache and went to see the ENT doctor. He checked me over and gave me a prescription for Ceftin. I had that medication on several previous occasions and it didn't bother me. This time was different. I left the prescription at the pharmacy at lunchtime to be filled with the intention of picking it up on my way home from work. While dinner was cooking I decided to take the pill and then eat. I sat down in the den with the TV on and took the pill with a glass of water. Within seconds, I noticed my throat felt as though it was closing. I then noticed my tongue felt as though it was swelling. I thought I had better get another glass of water and try sipping it to keep my throat from closing altogether. By the time I did this, my tongue was swollen to almost fill the entire cavity of my mouth. My throat was not entirely closed but I couldn't talk because of the swollen tongue. This went on for about a half hour or more. I then thought that I had better lie down. I decided to put on my night clothes and go to bed. When I removed my clothing my entire body, except my face and hands, was full of huge red welts. I later found out these were hives, yes an extreme case of hives. I went to bed and fell asleep. In the morning, my tongue was back to normal, and so was everything else including the hives were gone. Several months later I had a sinus infection and went to see our family doctor. He told me he was going to give me a prescription, and I asked him to not give me the same one as the ENT doctor had given me. I told him what had transpired and immediately he came over to where I was sitting on the examining table, and asked me if I knew how close I came to dying. I told him I knew it was serious, but not dying. He asked why we didn't call 911, they would have come and given me something to stop the problem. He told me never take that medication again or I wouldn't have time to pick up the phone and dial 911 because I would be dead. He then told me something that I will also never forget. He said, "this may surprise you." "When a doctor prescribes a medication of any kind for a patient he/she has no idea how the patient will react to the medication." "We just assume all will be well, and there will not be any complications because of the prescription." That was a total surprise to me and I told him so. He also said that he could write the same prescription eleven times in a row for the same patient with no problems. But on the 12th time, there would be disastrous consequences. There's no way of knowing. Now, that's something to remember! I guess if you really think about it though, it does make sense. We're all different. No matter, it happened to me and I thank God for taking care of me, and making sure I made it through that "could-have-been a disaster".

PRECOGNITION, WHAT'S THAT?

I didn't really know what that was until I was in my 30's. I had always had feelings and could actually tell and see things that were about to happen then or soon. My Mom had this same gift and so did my Grandmother. I think you can call it a gift as sometimes I was able to keep myself, family or friends from great harm. I would like to relate a few of these happenings to you now.

I found out it is called Precognition. When I was a small child it was almost as though I could read minds under certain circumstances. I remember some people would pat me on the head and say what a lovely child I was. I would look at them and then think to myself, why are they saying that because they really are thinking I'm a brat. Naturally, I never said that to anyone.

One of the first instances that comes vividly to mind was a car ride in which, my boyfriend (who is now my husband), my friend Janice and myself were travelling. It was the 4th of July and we three had been at the beach, and were driving Janice back to her Aunt's house. Jan and I were both 16 at the time. My boyfriend's front seat was a bench seat and so the three of us sat in the front. My friend was seated next to the passenger door, I in the middle, and Larry driving, of course. We were in a jolly mood having had a wonderful day at the beach. All of a sudden I knew we were going to get in an accident at the next corner. I screamed and started crying, and told Larry to please stop the car and not go any further. He pulled over to the side of the road and tried to calm me down. He promised me he would drive slowly and carefully, but I was not to be consoled. I begged him to stay where we were but he again promised to be careful. I finally relented and so he continued to drive. My heart was pounding as we entered the next intersection and suddenly we were hit by a car driven by a group of young people. Our car spun around 180 degrees. We couldn't get out of the passenger door as that's where they hit the car. The young people had been to a 4th of July party and had been drinking. They were travelling at a high rate of speed in the lane next to the curb, and didn't see our car until it was too late. My friend hit the side window and broke her nose. From the momentum of the swinging car, I tore all the muscle and tissue away from the bone in my right shoulder. My arm was in a sling for about 3 weeks. To this day I can't put my right arm above my head or my shoulder pops out. Larry was not hurt except that this was his new car which he had purchased just 4 days previous. He was very upset to say the least. It was now my turn to console him.

After Larry and I were married we had two boys as you have previously read. As they grew up they got used to me telling them to be careful. When things I would tell them were going to happen and they did, they would tell me I made it happen. Some of the things that I warned about were simple things like "Be careful backing up the car, you are going to hit a tree". When that did in fact happen our Son, Larry was not too happy with me, he thought I made it happen.

When Patrick was 14 I thought it would be great fun if he took Scuba lessons as his best friend wanted to do so as well. So for his birthday we gave him Scuba lessons. He was so excited and was having a ball. One Sunday near the end of his lessons, the instructor took the class on a beach dive. I was doing my usual household chores and not the least bit concerned about anything. I remember I was making the bed and all of a sudden I felt like I was drowning. I couldn't catch my breath and couldn't breathe. I knew Patrick was going to drown. I saw it happening like a movie playing in front of me, I could see him going down the anchor chain and he lost his mouthpiece and couldn't find it and he started to take in great gulps of water. I started to cry as there was nothing I could do. I paced the floor the rest of the day crying and wringing my hands. About 5:30 pm the phone rang and Patrick asked me to come pick up he and his friend at the scuba shop. I was so relieved and gladly agreed. I was especially relieved because up to that point, if I felt or saw something that was going to happen it always did. When I got to the Scuba shop he and Shelby came out all happy and laughing. When they got in the car I asked him how the dive went. He said the water was too rough and the instructor wouldn't let them go into the water, but the next weekend they were going to Catalina Island on a dive. I was devastated as I knew right then that the incident was going to happen on the dive near Catalina Island. He told me he had to have his money into the instructor by the next Wednesday. As the days went by he kept asking me about going to pay for the trip. I kept putting him off. Finally, he said to me, "Mom, what's wrong". I finally told him what I had seen and felt. He was quite shaken because he also knew my premonitions (if you want to call them that) always happened. However, by Wednesday the instructor called and asked if we were going to come pay for his ticket. I reluctantly agreed to go to the Scuba shop. When we got there I wrote out the check and handed it to the gentleman. He looked at me questioningly, and asked what was wrong. Patrick spoke up and said that his Mom could tell when something bad was going to happen and I didn't want him to go. He asked me what it was that was supposed to happen, and so I told him. He was shocked, and promptly told Patrick he would not take him on the trip. Patrick got quite upset so finally the instructor said, ok I'll take you but you don't move 2 inches away from my side at all times. Patrick agreed. The night before the big trip I couldn't sleep and so paced the floors half the night. Suddenly, about 3 o'clock in the morning a total calm overtook me, and I knew everything was going to be all right. When Patrick got up at 6:oo am to get ready to go, I told him I knew he would be o.k. He was much relieved to say the least. I picked up Shelby, his friend and diving partner in the car, and we made our way to the Scuba shop. I told Patrick to tell the instructor all would be well and so he did.

The instructor said he didn't care, Patrick and Shelby were still not allowed to leave his side. The trip to Catalina was great but when they dropped anchor everyone was allowed to jump in the water except Patrick and Shelby, they had to sit on the deck by the instructor. Finally, it was time to start doing the final test. About halfway through the group, the instructor told Patrick and Shelby it was their turn for the test. Patrick, Shelby and the instructor started down the anchor chain. When they reached the bottom they all walked a short distance from the chain to a spot where the testing would commence. After a few procedures, the instructor motioned for Shelby to take out his mouthpiece and pass it to Patrick as part of the test. Shelby shook his head no. The instructor motioned for him to remove his mouthpiece again, and Shelby shook his head no. The instructor unexpectedly pulled the mouthpiece out of Shelby's mouth. Shelby totally panicked and started taking in great gulps of water. The instructor tried to push in on his stomach to see if he could get any of the water out. When this did not work, he hurriedly assisted Shelby back to the anchor chain and brought him back up on board. He had to get the water out of his lungs, so he had Shelby lie on the deck so he could pump out the water. Fortunately, he was able to get most of the water out. Patrick asked if he was going to be tested, and the instructor said no. Patrick had done enough while they were down so the instructor didn't want to take any more chances. He went on to test the balance of the group and then allowed everyone to do a little snorkeling until time to start back to the mainland. Patrick and Shelby went into the water, but Shelby wasn't feeling well at all so they just came back on deck until the boat left to go back to the mainland. I didn't know any of this until I got the call from Patrick to come pick he and Shelby up at the shop. While he was on the phone he sounded strangely subdued, and asked me to put the backseat down in the station wagon. I expected him to be happy and excited, so his manner seemed unusual. However, I put the backseat down and started off for the shop. When I got to the parking lot out came the instructor and Patrick holding up Shelby. I opened the door and Shelby climbed into the back and lay down. When Patrick got in the car I asked what happened. He put his finger to his lips and quietly said shhh, and told me he would tell me later. When we got to Shelby's house he helped him into the house and then came back and got in the car. I asked him again what on earth had happened. He said, remember what you told me was going to happen to me on the dive, I answered yes, well he said it happened to Shelby instead. I reminded him that I had told him earlier that morning before we left that he would be all right, that nothing was going to happen to him. He told me how Shelby panicked when the mouthpiece was taken out of his mouth by the instructor, and he started to take in a great deal of water. Fortunately the instructor was right there and could help Shelby as he "totally lost it" according to Patrick. The instructor tried to push in on his stomach down below and get some of the water out. When this did not work he quickly got Shelby back toward the anchor chain, helped him up the chain and pulled him onto the deck. Although the instructor was surprised at Shelby's reaction to the mouthpiece being removed from his mouth, tragedy was averted as the instructor had been forewarned and was on the lookout for any kind of trouble. Thank you again Lord for the insight.

When we went to the shop to actually pick up Patrick's certificate a few days later, the instructor was somewhat rude. He said to me "Mrs. Thomas, I like you as a person but I never want to see you again". And we never went back.

Another Incident:

Son Larry was about 18 when he was introduced to a very influential young man here in our area. This young man's family owned a great deal of property in the hills and was very wealthy. Larry and his friend started to spend a great deal of time with this young man. One night shortly after I fell asleep I had a very disturbing dream. Our son was riding in a vehicle and was involved in an accident in which his face was hurt very badly. The next day when I woke up and saw him, I related my dream to him and told him to be very careful while riding in any vehicles. He took my warning rather casually as he always did, and said he would. Several nights later (about 3:00 o'clock in the morning) the phone rang by my side of the bed. I knew what it was before I answered it. The person on the other end of the line was the young man with whom son, Larry and his friend had become well acquainted. It seems the young man had been driving his pickup truck around the hills with the two guys in the back bed. He swerved around a tree with a low hanging branch. Our son was sitting in the very back of the bed of the truck near the tailgate. The young man hit the low hanging branch and it swung forward and then backward and hit our son in the face and knocked him out of the truck. You can imagine what his face looked like. He had a broken nose, eyes practically closed from the swelling, cuts, bruises and loose teeth. I felt so sorry for him, but I never reminded him of my dream and his response to my warning. It was too late for that.

<u>Another Incident</u>:

It was Friday morning and I was just awakening from sleep. The alarm had gone off at 7:00 am as usual as it was a work day, but I was very comfortable, not quite awake yet. I hadn't opened my eyes but finally thought I had better do just that. Suddenly I got a picture in my mind of a car accident. The automobile was turned over and all I could see was the bottom of the car and the wheels spinning. I couldn't tell who was in the car, what kind of a car it was or even the color. But I knew, I just knew it was someone in my family, and it was going to happen. I didn't know when, but it was going to be very soon. After I got up Larry told me he had to go to my cousin's house that day. My heart turned to ice. I thought it must be him. I practically begged him not to go. He got a little irritated with me and asked why not. I told him what I had seen. He was thoughtful, and he promised me he would be very careful driving. I told him to call me at work when he was leaving, when he arrived, when he left, and when he got back home. Thankfully, he did just that. I worried about it all day long at work, and waited, waited for the phone to ring. I was beside myself that I wasn't given enough information this time to be able to know who was going to have this accident. Usually my Precognition works so well, and I'm given pretty much all the details. This time, not so. I couldn't call my sons as they work and can't really receive calls at work. So I had no way of warning them. It was a harrowing day. By evening I relaxed a little as no one had called me of an accident. But I knew it wasn't over, it was going to happen to someone in the family but I didn't know who or when. We went to bed and I was surprised I slept at all. The next morning, Saturday, I received a call from our Son, Patrick around 10:00 am. He sounded o.k. but not like himself. The first thing he asked me was had I had any pre-warning of an accident. I said yes, and told him what I had seen. He then told me he and his wife, Cindy were at the hospital in Mission Viejo as our granddaughter had been in a horrendous accident. The previous late evening she and a group of friends decided to go out and get a snack. The group split up into couples, there were 5 cars. Heather didn't have a date so they paired her up with the only single fellow in the group. They left and decided to take a canyon route to the restaurant. It was a winding road, very dark-and very dangerous. Many accidents happen on that road. She and the young man were the lead car. He was younger than Heather and I think he was trying to impress her. He sped up going over 100 mph. He lost control of the car and almost hit a tree. In avoiding the tree he turned the steering wheel too hard, and the car flew across the street, hit an embank-ment, flipped into the air and rolled 3 times in the air. The car came down and rolled over 2 more times finally resting on the framework of the roof. The roof had been torn off in one of the rolls but the window frames were intact. Heather had put her left hand through the windshield and it was very seri-ously injured. The car finally came to rest on what was left of the roof, literally upside down. Both of them crawled out of the broken driver window and collapsed on the ground. This is what I had seen only I didn't know it was going to be Heather. Their friends who watched this horrific accident called 911 and the police arrived very quickly along with one or more ambulances. Both youngsters were taken to the nearest hospital that had a trauma center. The doctors did as much as they could surgically to repair Heather's left hand. She wound up having several more surgeries and more than two years of physical therapy. The young man had a concussion as did Heather, but he was able to leave the hospital fairly quickly. I keep wondering why I wasn't given enough information to warn Heather. Usually I know all the details. The doctor told both of the youngsters that it was a miracle they were alive. Heather has been a gymnast since she was 7. Unfortunately, this accident put a big damper on that activity for a number of years. She still has difficulty using her left hand but maybe with more surgeries and therapy one day she will. She did tell me recently that her hand will never be exactly as it once was. I believe more surgeries are planned, and we are hopeful these will enable her to get back to her gymnastics and other activities. She has limited use of her fingers and her wrist is still locked and she can't bend it at all. I keep wishing I had been able to warn her, however, maybe it wouldn't have mattered - it was going to happen regardless, and most probably she wouldn't have believed me anyway. She's at that age that her uncle Larry was when he found it hard to believe me. However, we do thank God that both she and the young man are alive. As the doctor told them both in the hospital, it was a miracle they were alive!

The one thing to know about my Precognition is that I have no control over it. Sometimes I am given information about something that is going to happen. I'm truly grateful as most of the time it's something very unpleasant that is going to happen to me or my family, and I can help prevent it or lessen the effect . Thank you Lord for this gift.

FIRE, FIRE!

S on Larry worked the night shift for a very large nation-wide company. He went to bed everyday around noon and got up at 8:00 pm to go to work. He worked until 6:00 am and then came home, relaxed, ate, went back to bed and the cycle started all over again, usually without incident. One day a few years ago, he followed his regular routine of going to bed at noon. He says he doesn't know what woke him up about 3:00 pm but something did. Upon getting up, he noticed his small fan quit running and so he got out of bed to check for the problem. As he went into the hallway from the bedroom, he heard a crackling sound coming from his son's bedroom. The door was closed and he decided to open it and investigate the noise. When he opened the door a wall of flames met his eyes. He had just gotten out of bed and had no shoes on, but he ran into the room and grabbed the blanket off the burning bed and tried to put out the flames. Practically everything in the room was on fire but he tried anyway. He made no headway, so he ran outside to the bedroom window, pushed the air conditioner through the opening and grabbing a hose tried to put out the fire that way. It was to no avail. He ran back inside the house and tried putting it out again. The smoke was getting thicker and it was getting harder to see and breathe. He ran outside one more time, and then back in again looking for his dog. By this time the smoke was so thick he had to feel his way using the walls as a guide to find the door to get out. At this same time, the mail person saw the smoke as he/she was coming down the street and called 911. The fire engines were there in a short time. They broke all the windows to let out the smoke, and even climbed on the roof to bore holes to let out as much smoke as possible. The firemen found the dog on the bedroom floor, it had expired in the smoke and fire. Larry Paul was taken to the hospital for smoke inhalation, cuts, and 3rd degree burns. Husband Larry went to pick him up from the hospital late that night. The next day his wife, Shauna called to tell me about the fire. They only rented the house they lived in, but there was a small (and I mean small) apartment of sorts over the garage which my grandson rented. After all

the fire engines and police left, the family had to stay somewhere for the night. They all went upstairs to the small apartment and slept on the floor. Grandson Larry didn't really live
in the garage apartment, he only used it for his computer
work and to entertain friends. He stayed in the house every
night because his Dad asked him to stay in the house. Since
Larry worked all night he didn't want to worry about Shauna
being by herself alone in the house. The arrangement was
made for that reason. As Shauna was telling me about the
fire, she told me of a strange thing that happened during the
night while they were all asleep upstairs. Sometime in the
middle of the night she woke up "for some reason", she said
she didn't know why. When she opened her eyes she saw
orange flickering on the walls and ceiling. She woke Larry
and they looked out of the window which faces the back
of the house. The pile of debris left from the fire between
the house and the steps to the garage apartment was on fire.
They ran down the wooden stairs and taking a hose Larry
put out the fire once again. When they were telling me of
this, I looked at them and said, you don't know what woke
you up, twice. I think you'd all better thank God for saving
you all. He saved Larry once, and then all of you again in
the middle of the night. That second fire between the house

and garage was only about 4 feet from the wooden stairs leading up to the garage apartment. Had that stairway and possibly the garage itself caught fire, there's no telling how this would have ended.

They thanked God for His help, and we did also. We could have lost all of them at one time but God protected them, and for that we are more than grateful.

The people in the neighborhood were wonderful. People came over to help take smoke covered clothes, etc. out of the house and to the dump. They brought food and drinks over for their breakfast, lunch and dinner. Some neighbor even brought over a couple of mattresses so they could sleep on them up in the garage apartment. The people, where Larry works took a collection not once but twice, and the company also gave him 2 checks to help with the tragedy. His son, Larry Jr. lost everything but the clothes he wore to work. Fortunately he had his computer in the garage apartment, a table and a few lamps. I believe he also had some dress clothes in the closet, however most of his clothing, shoes, etc. were lost in the fire. They had no renter's insurance so nothing was covered. Larry and Shauna did manage to get some clothing out of the house, and I spent 12 hours washing them. I had to sort them on the side porch as I couldn't stand the smell of smoke on everything they brought over. I didn't dare bring it into the house. Larry needed to have skin grafts on his arms and hands due to the 3rd degree burns. But all things considered, they are very fortunate they all had the help of God to keep them alive.

Something very interesting, Larry said he never felt any pain from the cuts and 3rd degree burns. The doctors in the hospital wanted to give him pain pills but he told them he didn't need them as he didn't have any pain. They could hardly believe it. With all the cuts and burns they said he should be in a great deal of pain. He can't believe it, they couldn't believe it and we find it hard to believe. You probably do too, however, the Lord works in mysterious ways, and I'm sure this is the way the Lord wanted it, and we are all grateful for it.

BITE YOUR TONGUE

G randson, Larry has a job working at a shop for a gentleman who repairs wave runners, jet skis motor-cycles, etc. They make sure the items are working prop-erly after the repairs by testing. One day they traveled to Catalina Island to test several wave runners. They were on their way back about 6 miles off of Long Beach when a very distressing incident happened. Larry was testing one of the wave runners traveling about 60 miles an hour. Suddenly his finger slipped off of the throttle as he went into a big wave. The wave runner stopped suddenly. That threw him forward causing his face to hit the handle bars. He hit his face below his nose, and unknowingly bit through his tongue almost severing it. The whole movement threw him forward and he fell over the craft into the water. Fortunately there was another craft behind him that stopped and he crawled up and got on board. He didn't realize he had bit his tongue that severely. Once on the other craft it became apparent he had, as he said, "it was like a waterfall of blood flowing out of his mouth." His friend who had picked him up tried to calm him down, and tried not to alarm him as to the severity of his injury. He sat for about 10 minutes to regain his composure, and then they continued on toward shore As they drove back the salt water helped to stem the bleeding. Once back on shore they loaded the equipment back on the truck, and it was suggested to Larry that he go to the Urgent Care Center. The Center took one look at his injury and told him to go to the hospital. Once at the hospital, they stuffed his mouth with gauze and put tubes in his throat as he couldn't breathe very well because of the amount of blood in his mouth and throat. The doctor said he had lost a lot of blood. They called an ENT to do the surgery to repair his tongue. The ENT told him later that his tongue had been holding practically by a thread. His tongue was so swollen he could barely swallow. For a month or more, he was on a liquid diet as his tongue was so swollen he couldn't move it to chew. It was very distressing for months because he couldn't taste any food or drink once he could eat again. He had no feeling on the end of his tongue for months. It was approximately 3 months before he began to have any feeling in his tongue, and able to actually taste food and drink. He worried because he thought he might never be able to taste food or drink again or actually feel his tongue. It was very difficult to talk as well as that requires moving your mouth and tongue.

So all around it was quite an experience he hadn't expected. But the family is very grateful he didn't drown that day and that he is back to his normal self. I believe Larry, Jr. himself came to realize that God saved him from a great disaster that day. He is most grateful as well. He is also super careful when testing any of the equipment now. No Repeats Please!

A BIG THANK YOU

To all of you who have purchased this book and read it, I thank you. Above all though, I am hoping that it brought to light some instances in your life that just can't quite be explained in a logical way. Almighty God does not always work in logical ways. You've heard this quite a few times, God has a plan for each and everyone of us. Thankfully He sees to it that the plan works no matter how we try to side step along the way. Please be sure and thank Him for all those times He could have looked the other way, and disaster may not have been averted. I think there are probably times when God does look the other way and lets us make decisions that are not in our best interest. In a way you can be thankful for that as we do learn from our mistakes, as the saying goes. I'm glad that God loves me anyway. I'm sure you feel the same way yourself. After reading this book, I'm sure you can see for yourself how God has looked out for me and my family – that's what you call unconditional love! It's precious and special!

My hope is that you all enjoyed the book and found something in it to bring into your life. God Bless!

AND THAT'S WHAT'S HAPPENED

TO RATSY PATSY AND HER FAMILY . . . .

SO FAR!